Once upon a

CAMPUS

Once upon a CAMPUS

TRENT ANDERSON AND SEPPY BASILI

KAPLAN

published by Simon & Schuster

New York   London   Toronto   Sydney   Singapore

Kaplan Publishing
Published by Simon & Schuster, Inc.
1230 Avenue of the Americas
New York, NY 10020

For bulk sales to schools, colleges, and universities, please contact: Order Department, Simon & Schuster, Inc., 100 Front Street, Riverside, NJ 08075. Phone: (800) 223-2336. Fax: (800) 943-9831.

For information regarding special discounts for other bulk purchases, please contact Simon & Schuster Special Sales at 1-800-456-6798 or business@simonandschuster.com

Cover Design: Bradford Foltz
Cover Illustration: Scott Ritchie
Interior Design: Lisa Stokes
Editor: Beth Grupper

Manufactured in the United States of America

May 2003
10 9 8 7 6 5 4 3 2 1

Library of Congress Cataloging-in-Publication Data
ISBN 0-7432-4933-X

I would like to thank my family and my friends, for all the support in the form of long-distance phone calls that I received while working on this project. A special thank you to my roommate, Karen, for your help on getting that first difficult chapter finished. Finally, my sincere thanks to Maureen McMahon for giving me my first job opportunity out of college.

–Supurna Banerjee

The publisher would like to thank Colin Shields for his contribution to this project.

ACKNOWLEDGMENTS

CONTENTS

Hi, we're Trent and Seppy. This book will give you the inside scoop on how to survive and thrive in college. We've searched the country for the best advice from current college students and recent grads about how to make college fun, exciting, and rewarding. They've lived and learned, and now you get to benefit from their wisdom—and learn from their mistakes. We guarantee 100 percent that the advice in this book will be unbiased and straightforward and that it will help you succeed in college (if not, the book makes a great coaster).*

We'll be popping in every now and then with survival tips: notes, suggestions, and our expert advice. Why should you listen to us? We've both worked with thousands of students, helping them with admissions, test prep, and financial aid advice. Our comments are based on our own experience and what we've learned by speaking to students and college personnel throughout the years.

We hope you enjoy this book—however you decide to use it. Now that we've exchanged introductions, you're ready to discover how *Once Upon a Campus* . . . students went to college and lived to tell about it.

Trent Anderson   **Seppy Basili**

*Claims of a "guarantee" for success in college or use of this book as a "coaster" have not been confirmed by any valid authority.

1

READY, SET, GO!

Don't expect to recognize yourself four years from now.

GRADUATE, ENGLISH/PSYCHOLOGY, VASSAR COLLEGE

THE BEST FOUR YEARS OF YOUR LIFE

READY, SET, GO!

You'll forget the formulas you learn in Calculus and the wars you learn about in History, but you'll never forget the memories you make with your friends in college.

GRADUATE, BIOMETRY/STATISTICS, CORNELL UNIVERSITY

College is really the only time in your life when you essentially have no responsibilities other than to go to school and pay rent. Enjoy it.

GRADUATE, INTERNATIONAL STUDIES/RUSSIAN, JOHNS HOPKINS UNIVERSITY

Every day at college is amazing—you get to live with your friends and do things you enjoy. IT'S A GREAT LIFE; TAKE ADVANTAGE OF EVERY SINGLE MOMENT.

SENIOR, RHETORIC AND COMMUNICATION STUDIES, UNIVERSITY OF RICHMOND

Take risks. GO OUT ON A LIMB. Don't be afraid to do things you, your friends, and maybe even your family don't think you're capable of. Put everything on the line so you can find out what you're really capable of and who you really are.

SENIOR, PHILOSOPHY, ST. JOHN'S COLLEGE (ANNAPOLIS)

It's important to take time and **be the stereotype . . .** *dye your hair blue, be a pseudo-hippie, protest stuff . . . it'll never be as socially acceptable as it is now.*

GRADUATE, BIOCHEMISTRY AND CELL BIOLOGY, UNIVERSITY OF CALIFORNIA—SAN DIEGO

Among entering freshmen "participation in organized demonstrations . . . reached an all-time high 47.5 percent in 2001."

Sax, Linda J., et al. "The American Freshman: National Norms for Fall 2001." Cooperative Institutional Research Program. 2001.

Be true to yourself and live like there is no tomorrow.

SENIOR, PHILOSOPHY, COLLEGE OF WILLIAM & MARY

Find yourself. It'll be the most important thing you'll learn.

SENIOR, PSYCHOLOGY, UNIVERSITY OF ILLINOIS—CHICAGO

WORK HARD BUT HAVE FUN. YOU ONLY GET TO DO THIS ONCE.

JUNIOR, BIOMEDICAL ENGINEERING, SAINT LOUIS UNIVERSITY

You'll meet many different types of people in college. Take advantage of the freedom to express who you are, and learn from those who are different from you.

GRADUATE, ECONOMICS/COMMUNICATIONS, UNIVERSITY OF PENNSYLVANIA

College is the best place to approach new experiences since you have virtually no responsibilities compared to the "real world." **BE SURE TO MAKE THAT FREEDOM WORTHWHILE.**

GRADUATE, PHYSIOLOGY/PSYCHOLOGY, UNIVERSITY OF MICHIGAN

I COULDN'T HAVE MADE IT THROUGH COLLEGE WITHOUT . . .

My CD collection.

SENIOR, GERMAN/PSYCHOLOGY, UNIVERSITY OF FLORIDA

The Internet. It's priceless—you can use it for research, procrastinating, communicating with friends . . . the list goes on and on.

SENIOR, ANTHROPOLOGY, UNIVERSITY OF TORONTO

My five-subject notebook—it's much easier than carrying multiple notebooks and you never grab the wrong one.

GRADUATE, LEGAL STUDIES, UNIVERSITY OF MASSACHUSETTS—AMHERST

My friends. I wouldn't have wanted to.

GRADUATE, ENGLISH, CORNELL UNIVERSITY

RAMEN NOODLES and Coca-Cola!!!

GRADUATE, SPEECH-LANGUAGE PATHOLOGY, TOWSON UNIVERSITY

2

NEW PLACES, NEW FACES, AND NAME GAMES

Be that person who embarrasses himself on the first day of orientation. Everyone will remember, and from that day forward you will have an icebreaker.

GRADUATE, PSYCHOLOGY, COLBY-SAWYER COLLEGE

A CLEAN SLATE

The best part of freshman orientation was making a fresh start.

GRADUATE, CRIMINAL JUSTICE,
STATE UNIVERSITY OF NEW YORK—UNIVERSITY AT ALBANY

I got to reinvent myself and find new people to be friends with.

SENIOR, PSYCHOLOGY, UNIVERSITY OF SAN FRANCISCO

The best part was seeing all the new sights and exploring all the possibilities.

JUNIOR, NEUROSCIENCE, UNIVERSITY OF PITTSBURGH

SEPPY'S SURVIVAL TIP

Get lost . . . on campus. Letting yourself wander aimlessly will help once classes start and you need to find how to get from Intro to Chemistry to Philosophy 101.

The worst part of freshman orientation was realizing that I was totally alone and starting from ground zero. I spent those nights crying under trees on campus, knowing that I had led myself far from home and into a world where I was a blank slate.

GRADUATE, PSYCHOLOGY/UNIVERSITY SCHOLARS PROGRAM, XAVIER UNIVERSITY

The worst part of freshman orientation was the statistics! Don't get swallowed up in "only 18 percent of students get As and 40 percent get a C average during freshman year." Study hard and believe in yourself.

SENIOR, PSYCHOLOGY/PRE-MEDICINE, UNIVERSITY OF IOWA

TRENT'S SURVIVAL TIP

Some colleges also offer pre-registration to entering freshmen. Find out your registration options by reading the information you receive over the summer or by calling the registrar's office.

The worst part of orientation was . . . the incredibly long line at registration. Online registration is the best thing ever!

JUNIOR, BIOMEDICAL SCIENCES, UNIVERSITY OF SOUTH ALABAMA

The best and worst part of freshman orientation was the boring speeches. But they proved valuable to me later on.

SENIOR, PSYCHOLOGY, UNIVERSITY OF ALABAMA—HUNTSVILLE

Everything is thrown at you at once and it feels very overwhelming, but you are not asked to know everything right away. Just know that they are exposing you to as many things as possible to get you excited about the school.

GRADUATE, BIOLOGY, UNIVERSITY OF CENTRAL FLORIDA

IT'S A REAL PARADOX, the orientation experience, because although it was miserable and seemed pointless, it definitely made a lasting impact. And being in a new place where I didn't know a single person, those ridiculous "getting-to-know-you" games helped me make some connections with people. I needed to know that I wasn't alone.

GRADUATE, ART AND DESIGN, LAGRANGE COLLEGE

ORIENTATION TIPS

Seppy Says:

Orientation's really important for a couple of reasons. First, it gives you a chance to establish networks. Right when you get on campus, seek out the older students you know from your high school. You can get the real lowdown on teachers from them, as well as notes or outlines from previous years.

Second, orientation gives you a chance to figure out how you're going to want to study and work before classes are in full swing. It's best to try and start with a plan rather than trying to come up with one in the middle of the semester.

Trent Says:

Hold off on the shopping sprees until after orientation, because what you need may be different than what you initially thought you wanted. Especially wait on big purchases, like a computer. Most people buy computers that are different in some way than what they need (e.g., ethernet vs. cable, Windows XP vs. Windows ME).

A note on unofficial orientation activities: You've got four years to go out and party. The first few weeks of school are *not* the time to do it.

THE WORST PART ABOUT FRESHMAN ORIENTATION WAS . . .

Playing Twister in dog food and then having a senior throw eggs at us. EW, shower!

SENIOR, SOCIAL WORK, NIAGARA UNIVERSITY

Icebreakers and duck-duck-goose.

SENIOR, NEUROSCIENCE, UNIVERSITY OF ROCHESTER

Being led around like cattle in 90-degree heat.

GRADUATE, COGNITIVE SCIENCE, UNIVERSITY OF VIRGINIA

When I spilled cranberry juice all over my orientation leader.

GRADUATE, BIOLOGY, SAINT JOSEPH'S UNIVERSITY

Having to say my name, where I was from, and which dorm I lived in *soooo* many times.

SENIOR, RHETORIC AND COMMUNICATIONS STUDIES, UNIVERSITY OF RICHMOND

THE BEST PART ABOUT FRESHMAN ORIENTATION WAS . . .

The silly games we played.

GRADUATE, NEAR EASTERN AND JUDAIC STUDIES, BRANDEIS UNIVERSITY

Getting my college ID, which made me feel like I was really in college.

GRADUATE, SOCIOLOGY/POLITICAL SCIENCE, STATE UNIVERSITY OF NEW YORK—UNIVERSITY AT BUFFALO

How much help and support I got right on the first day.

GRADUATE, ZOOLOGY/PRE-MEDICINE, CONNECTICUT COLLEGE

Meeting all the new people and realizing I wasn't alone.

SENIOR, SOCIOLOGY/ECONOMICS, UNIVERSITY OF MASSACHUSETTS—AMHERST

The glow on my face the whole time . . . I was so happy.

GRADUATE, PUBLIC RELATIONS, UNIVERSITY OF FLORIDA

3 FREE AT LAST . . . NOW WHAT?

*Freedom is like a gallon of ice cream—you don't want to
eat all of it at once and never eat it again.*

SENIOR, POLITICAL SCIENCE/CHINESE LANGUAGE,

UNIVERSITY OF CALIFORNIA—IRVINE

I can do what I want when I want. *It doesn't matter if I feel like going to get a Slurpee from 7-Eleven at 3 A.M. . . . I don't have to ask permission.*

SENIOR, BIOLOGY, MARY WASHINGTON COLLEGE

I went a little crazy and got a rock star boyfriend who turned out to be trouble, but a good distraction.

SENIOR, JOURNALISM, UNIVERSITY OF TEXAS—AUSTIN

I drank a beer, got a belly-button ring, and just before Christmas break my freshman year, I got a tattoo. I still drink beer, I lost the belly-button ring, and, fortunately, my tattoo is in a very inconspicuous place. My political career will be safe.

GRADUATE, POLITICAL SCIENCE/ENGLISH, VIRGINIA POLYTECHNIC INSTITUTE AND STATE UNIVERSITY

Freedom is great until you need your family. I took off, went out all the time, never called home. But when you get sick, stressed out, or nervous and you need a comforting word, it's nice to have that connection.

SENIOR, NEUROSCIENCE, UNIVERSITY OF ROCHESTER

I did everything my parents told me not to do, made up my own mind about what I thought was right and wrong, and eventually came to the same conclusions as my parents. Funny, isn't it?

GRADUATE, BIOLOGY, COLLEGE OF CHARLESTON

It was great to get away from home. The sense of freedom and doing whatever you want helps you mature faster, I think, because your parents aren't there to push you. You just have to do what you feel is the right thing to do.

SENIOR, PRE-LAW/MASS COMMUNICATIONS, OHIO STATE UNIVERSITY

SACRIFICING YOUR GPA TO THE PARTY GODS

I went crazy the first semester of college. I didn't do well at all, especially since I was taking Chemistry and Trigonometry. It's really easy to get caught up in the partying. Don't let it get in the way of what you're in college for.

GRADUATE, ENGLISH, UNIVERSITY OF FLORIDA

At first I definitely went a little crazy, but after a while I realized what I needed to do and I did it. My freshman grades are what will probably keep me out of a great graduate school.

SENIOR, ACCOUNTING, UTAH STATE UNIVERSITY

The 2001 Harvard School of Public Health College Alcohol Study of students at 199 four-year colleges revealed that "in 2001, approximately 2 in 5 (44.4 percent) college students reported binge drinking." The study "defined binge drinking as the consumption of at least 5 drinks in a row for men or 4 drinks in a row for women during the 2 weeks before completion of the questionnaire."

Wechsler, Henry, et al. "Trends in College Binge Drinking During a Period of Increased Prevention Efforts: Findings from Four Harvard School of Public Health Study Surveys: 1993-2001." *Journal of American College Health.* March 2002.

When a friend's drinking gets out of control, you already know to keep his car keys in the fridge or some other place where he can't get to them. But you may not know that some methods people commonly use to sober up—cold showers, drinking coffee—can actually cause more harm than good. For more information about alcohol myths, intervention, and prevention, check out factsontap.org.

Be careful at parties. Drinking and going crazy is an inevitable and fun part of college, but never do anything you will regret. Also, watch out for your friends in those situations.

GRADUATE, BIOMEDICAL SCIENCES, MARQUETTE UNIVERSITY

ONCE UPON A CAMPUS

ALL WORK AND NO PLAY MAKES JACK A DULL BOY

little craziness never hurt anybody—unless you go down-right wild. Have fun, do things you've never done before, go to parties (you don't have to drink), go on dates. I personally loved "going out." You can't stay up till 2 A.M. forever, so enjoy it while it lasts! Some of my best memories are hanging out at a friend's apartment having a casual beverage, playing games, whatever.

GRADUATE, MASS COMMUNICATIONS, NORTHEASTERN STATE UNIVERSITY

I went crazy . . . most people go crazy, but then you realize what you are doing to your life and how much your tuition costs each year, and you shape up.

SENIOR, POLITICAL SCIENCE, INDIANA UNIVERSITY

I explore my surroundings and I spend time by myself during the day because I can. College is one of the only times in your life where you can spend three hours during the day reading in a coffee shop or at the student lounge.

SENIOR, ANTHROPOLOGY, UNIVERSITY OF TORONTO

Collegiate buddies soon become your urban family. Sometimes we do homey things like stay in and cook dinner or just chit-chat about home.

SENIOR, GENDER STUDIES/RELIGIOUS STUDIES, BROWN UNIVERSITY

I drove all over on the slightest whim. At 4 A.M. my friends and I drove to the Oregon coast, a two-hour drive, so we could greet the sunrise; we'd drive to Seattle, a four-hour drive, so we could go to a concert on a Friday night. We traveled everywhere and didn't ever sleep.

GRADUATE, BIOCHEMISTRY/MOLECULAR BIOLOGY, REED COLLEGE

When I was a freshman I used to stay out until all hours of the night (and early morning)—not even really doing much of anything—because I could! We made 3 A.M. runs to Denny's and Steak n Shake. But I made sure that if I did those spur-of-the-moment things I stayed up and did homework the next night.

SENIOR, BIOLOGY, OBERLIN COLLEGE

Exercise your newfound freedom moderately. If you overdo it, you'll be the one and only person taking away your freedom.

SENIOR, POLITICAL SCIENCE/CHINESE LANGUAGE, UNIVERSITY OF CALIFORNIA—IRVINE

I feel that the college experience helps merge young adults into the real world. **During my freshman year in college I was faced with paying numerous bills, balancing my checkbook, doing my own laundry, and cooking and cleaning.**

SENIOR, PSYCHOLOGY/CRIMINOLOGY, FLORIDA STATE UNIVERSITY

Once I had the freedom I had been longing for, I found out that there really was not much that I wanted to do that I had not been able to do before.

GRADUATE, ECONOMICS, UNIVERSITY OF ALABAMA—TUSCALOOSA

4

HOME, SWEET HOME

If you can make it through one year in the smallest room ever, you will appreciate every other place you live for the rest of your life.

SENIOR, MARKETING, UNIVERSITY OF NOTRE DAME

OPEN UP YOUR MIND. You're going to experience and see things you never even imagined, and you need to be prepared for very odd things.

SENIOR, ENGLISH/CREATIVE WRITING AND FILM/PHOTOGRAPHY, HOLLINS UNIVERSITY

Dorm life is what you make of it. You uncover your niche, whether it be in the hall where you live or the sorority/fraternity/academic club/sport you choose. This isn't high school anymore—it's not embarrassing to be who you are and do what you like.

GRADUATE, SOCIAL RELATIONS, JAMES MADISON COLLEGE AT MICHIGAN STATE UNIVERSITY

COMPROMISE, COMPROMISE, COMPROMISE.

GRADUATE, PSYCHOLOGY, NEW YORK UNIVERSITY

Be aggressive. If people are being too loud in the dorms, have a plan. Talk to the RA, buy earplugs, do something. Don't assume that just because you live there, you have to take it.

Be flexible. People will be loud, annoying, irritating—just go with the flow and try not to let your feathers get ruffled.

SENIOR, NEUROSCIENCE, UNIVERSITY OF ROCHESTER

Realize that everyone in the dorm makes sacrifices to live together. Don't get bent out of shape about the little things—talk things out calmly and don't hold grudges.

GRADUATE, ART AND DESIGN, LAGRANGE COLLEGE

Don't sweat the small stuff . . . if you sweat them profusely, you'll go nuts (and probably dehydrate and die).

SENIOR, GENETICS, IOWA STATE UNIVERSITY

Find some place you can call your own. Suddenly you are living with a bunch of kids your age, none of whom really know you. IT CAN BE OVERWHELMING. Putting aside personal time and space becomes really important to your happiness.

GRADUATE, ENGLISH/FRENCH, CORNELL UNIVERSITY

TIPS ON HOUSING OPTIONS

Trent Says:

If there is a dorm that pre-screens people with similar interests, that often works out well. If it doesn't, you can always change dorms later. For many people, the most important part of college is just maturing as an individual. If you can find people with similar interests to help you along in the process, that's great. I'm a big advocate of that.

Seppy Says:

You might have the opportunity to live in theme housing, single-sex dorms, quiet dorms, or some other alternative housing option. Just keep in mind that you lock yourself in if you sign up for one of those. That said, it's a great way to help identify yourself, not unlike the way that people like to identify themselves with a fraternity or sorority. It's a way for you to develop an affinity or cohort that's natural. Still, I'd only recommend these housing options for students who are certain that they want to do it.

Be open and talk to your hall mates. Suppressing your inhibitions and fear of talking to the "stranger next door" is key to adjusting to dorm life, particularly when homesickness rears its head.

GRADUATE, SOCIOLOGY/POLITICAL SCIENCE, STATE UNIVERSITY OF NEW YORK—UNIVERSITY AT BUFFALO

Make friends on your hall. If you do, you will always be guaranteed to have someone to go to dinner with.

GRADUATE, BIOLOGY AND NUTRITION, PENNSYLVANIA STATE UNIVERSITY

Have friends outside your dorm. **Dorms, by the second month of school, tend to turn into soap operas.** You need a place where you can go hang out with friends who don't live with you.

GRADUATE, POLITICAL SCIENCE, SAINT JOSEPH'S UNIVERSITY

Make friends in your hall, but get involved in clubs so you are out and about and coming home feels like home—not a prison where you spend all your time.

GRADUATE, SOCIOLOGY/FAMILY STUDIES AND HUMAN DEVELOPMENT, UNIVERSITY OF ARIZONA

HOME, SWEET HOME

Stay away from "hall-cest" (hooking up with or dating someone in the same hall or dorm as you) if your hall is small. You will feel like you are married because that person is ALWAYS THERE!!! and it will be *bad* if you break up in the middle of the year, 'cause you will see the person ALL THE TIME!!!

SENIOR, BIOLOGY, OBERLIN COLLEGE

Remember that the people on your hall *don't* have to be your best friends. If you make your circle of friends out of only your dorm buddies, a disagreement within your hall can not only make your living situation hard, it can also mess with your social life. It's best to have friends from numerous places, like from your activities and classes, rather than from just your hall.

GRADUATE, ENGLISH/MUSIC, COLLEGE OF WILLIAM & MARY

Don't live with your good friends. You'll find out stuff about them that you wish you hadn't, and you might not end up being friends afterward.

SENIOR, PSYCHOLOGY, UNIVERSITY OF ILLINOIS—URBANA-CHAMPAIGN

GERM WARFARE

Wash your hands often. Although it sounds silly, it will help you stay healthy when others around you get sick.

GRADUATE, HEALTH AND SOCIETY, UNIVERSITY OF ROCHESTER

Wear flip-flops in the shower. YOU DON'T WANT WHAT GROWS IN THE SHOWER TO GROW ON YOUR FEET!

SENIOR, ENVIRONMENTAL DESIGN, TEXAS A&M UNIVERSITY—COLLEGE STATION

Think with your head when it comes to your health. Get hepatitis B and meningitis vaccinations.

GRADUATE, HISTORY, RUTGERS—THE STATE UNIVERSITY OF NEW JERSEY

You'll need duct tape for everything! No nails allowed in dorm walls—use duct tape to hang things! Need to stop your carpet from moving around—use duct tape! Anything you need to hold together, from your car to your backpack to your room, duct tape will fix much more cheaply than any alternative!

GRADUATE, PSYCHOLOGY/UNIVERSITY SCHOLARS PROGRAM, XAVIER UNIVERSITY

Have enough underwear to last the whole term, just in case you don't get around to doing laundry.

GRADUATE, GOVERNMENT, DARTMOUTH COLLEGE

The keys to surviving dorm life: patience, headphones, earplugs, and a bottle of echinacea/Vitamin C.

GRADUATE, EARLY CHILDHOOD AND ELEMENTARY EDUCATION, NEW YORK UNIVERSITY

Have earplugs and an eye mask so you can sleep at night, even when your roommate isn't.

GRADUATE, ENVIRONMENTAL STUDIES, EMORY & HENRY COLLEGE

DON'T FORGET TO PACK . . .

Downy Wrinkle Releaser and Shout Wipes—no ironing or washing.

GRADUATE, ECONOMICS, UNIVERSITY OF ALABAMA—TUSCALOOSA

More socks, you go through those like crazy!

GRADUATE, ENGINEERING SCIENCES, DARTMOUTH COLLEGE

Quarters . . . damn quarters!

GRADUATE, HISTORY, UNIVERSITY OF MASSACHUSETTS

A toolbox—you need a hammer and a screwdriver.

SENIOR, INTERNATIONAL BUSINESS, XAVIER UNIVERSITY

A dog to eat your homework.

SENIOR, EXERCISE AND MOVEMENT SCIENCE, UNIVERSITY OF OREGON

Note: Many retail stores and websites have special college sections to help students shop for essential college supplies. Check out *bedbathandbeyond.com, urbanoutfitters.com, kmart.com,* and *lnt.com* (Linens 'n Things), to help you get started.

5

THE GOOD, THE BAD, AND THE UGLY . . . ROOMMATE

I had a single (thank God).

GRADUATE, PSYCHOLOGY, UNIVERSITY OF CALIFORNIA—SAN DIEGO

THE GOOD, THE BAD, AND THE UGLY

Remember the #1 rule: If it would annoy you if your roommate did it, it will probably annoy your roommate if you do it.

GRADUATE, CHEMICAL ENGINEERING, UNIVERSITY OF VIRGINIA

ALL ROOMMATES ARE WEIRD. The key is realizing that your roommate is weird (and so are you) and deciding to get along with her anyway.

SENIOR, BIOLOGY, SEATTLE PACIFIC UNIVERSITY

Have an open mind. Unless your roommate is disrespectful, you have to realize that everybody is different and be willing to adjust to those differences.

JUNIOR, BIOLOGY, OHIO STATE UNIVERSITY

SEPPY'S SURVIVAL TIP

You have to use your own meter when deciding how ready you are to deal with sharing a room with someone. Just remember that the other person is going through some of the same things that you are—and she may never have had to share a room before.

Don't assume that what works for you will work for your roommate. As you will quickly learn, people come to college with all kinds of perspectives and from different backgrounds. Whether it's walking around the room naked or using his stuff without permission, he may feel differently than you about various issues. Always ask first.

GRADUATE, NEUROSCIENCE AND BEHAVIOR, WESLEYAN UNIVERSITY

I roomed with a girl I knew from home for the first two years of college. It greatly hindered me from getting to know new people. It gave me a sense of security, in that I knew someone from home, but it ended up pretty messy. Don't room with someone you already know!

GRADUATE, BIOLOGY, SAINT JOSEPH'S UNIVERSITY

A good roommate should never disrespect you, your things, or your opinions.

GRADUATE, PRE-MEDICINE, PENNSYLVANIA STATE UNIVERSITY

Students who are held in high esteem by their roommates are happier and have fewer problems than those who aren't. Roommates who aren't liked as much have more mental and physical problems, including depression and illness.

Joiner, T., K. Vohs, and N. B. Schmidt. "Social Appraisal as Correlate, Antecedent, and Consequence of Mental and Physical Health Outcomes." *Journal of Social and Clinical Psychology.* vol. 19. Fall 2000.

DON'T LEAVE YOUR MANNERS AT HOME

Never try to "mother" your roommate! I had a roommate who would try to regulate my naps and my schedule—it drove me crazy!!

GRADUATE, CRIMINAL JUSTICE, VITERBO UNIVERSITY

BE WILLING TO COMPROMISE WITH YOUR ROOMMATE. If she wants to have her boyfriend over and you can't stand him, talk to her about it and figure out a solution.

SENIOR, BIOMEDICAL SCIENCES, MARQUETTE UNIVERSITY

If you arrive before your roommate, do not choose your bed, drawers, or closet. Wait until your roommate arrives and then draw straws or flip a coin. **You never want to seem inconsiderate from Day One.**

GRADUATE, ENGLISH/FRENCH, CORNELL UNIVERSITY

SLEEP IS A HOT COMMODITY!

No roommate should ever interfere with her roommate's sleeping pattern. This includes never slamming the door when your roommate is sleeping, trying to keep the lights off as much as possible when you have to stay up late or wake up early, and discussing whether sleeping with the TV or radio on is okay with her.

GRADUATE, ENGLISH, TEXAS WOMEN'S UNIVERSITY

A good roommate should never assume that he knows what the other is thinking. Communication is vital in such a small space.

GRADUATE, HISTORY, UNIVERSITY OF MASSACHUSETTS

Don't hold a grudge. Little arguments can quickly become catastrophes when confined to closed spaces. Learn to forgive quickly.

GRADUATE, BIOCHEMISTRY, UNIVERSITY OF CALIFORNIA—DAVIS

Learn to speak up for yourself. Even if your roommates are wonderful, there are bound to be confrontations, and the only way to solve them is by learning to say what needs to be said in a constructive way.

SENIOR, PHILOSOPHY, STATE UNIVERSITY OF NEW YORK—UNIVERSITY AT ALBANY

ROOMMATE TIPS

Seppy Says:

If you have issues with your roommate, confront him right away. Some roommate conflicts are inevitable and you're probably not always going to get your way, so try to make a deal or compromise with your roommate. Confronting issues as they arise is always a really good way to go, and that's usually the hard part.

Trent Says:

Check out the official procedures at your school for dealing with roommate conflicts. If things are really bad, most schools have a process by which you can try to swap roommates or move.

Often the best thing to do is go to the RA. Having someone else mediate between you and your roommate can make a big difference. Some people get nervous and think that getting someone else involved would make things worse. Well, if it's that bad, it's not going to get any worse—and it definitely isn't going to get better unless you do something about it.

A good roommate would never put her roommate into any danger. I had a roommate who would bring men into the bedroom, completely intoxicated. She would leave them there and go back out. So I would wake up to some drunken stranger in my room.

GRADUATE, ECONOMICS, NEW YORK UNIVERSITY

A good roommate should never leave **DEFROSTING SHEEP HEARTS** in the fridge uncovered so they drip on your cans of Mountain Dew.

GRADUATE, BIOCHEMISTRY/CELL BIOLOGY, UNIVERSITY OF CALIFORNIA—SAN DIEGO

A good roommate should never use his roommate's dish scrubber to clean a neighbor's bathroom floor for money.

SENIOR, PSYCHOLOGY, ARIZONA STATE UNIVERSITY

ONCE UPON A CAMPUS

6

KEEPING YOURSELF AND YOUR STUFF SAFE

Use common sense. College campuses aren't much different than any other place.

SENIOR, POLITICAL SCIENCE, UNIVERSITY OF CALIFORNIA—SAN DIEGO

THE KEY TO SECURITY

Although you should be open to new ideas and people, your room shouldn't. Always lock it when you're not there.

SENIOR, LEGAL STUDIES, QUINNIPIAC UNIVERSITY

Lock your door, and threaten your roommate if she doesn't lock the door.

GRADUATE, ENGINEERING SCIENCES, DARTMOUTH COLLEGE

Always lock your door when you are away or sleeping. I can't even tell you how many stories I've heard about drunk people accidentally walking into the wrong room late at night.

GRADUATE, COGNITIVE SCIENCE, UNIVERSITY OF VIRGINIA

Carry pepper spray in your hand; it doesn't do any good in your backpack.

GRADUATE, PSYCHOLOGY, UNIVERSITY OF ILLINOIS—URBANA-CHAMPAIGN

Don't go jogging at night, especially not while wearing headphones. There are twenty-four hours in a day, twelve of which are during daylight—jog then and stay safe.

SENIOR, GOVERNMENT, UNIVERSITY OF VIRGINIA

Carry mace if you're out alone at night and call a friend while walking home so that if something were to happen, someone would know you were missing, where you were, and when it happened.

SENIOR, POLITICAL SCIENCE, UNIVERSITY OF CALIFORNIA—DAVIS

Never put yourself in a situation where no one knows where you are. If you didn't come home, how long would it be before anyone noticed?

GRADUATE, PSYCHOLOGY, UNIVERSITY OF ALABAMA

BETTER SAFE THAN SORRY

Be aware of the people around you at all times. Most campuses have police who will escort you on campus. Use this service if you feel the slightest concern for your safety. Get a cell phone and know their phone number and the phone number for roadside assistance.

GRADUATE, ENGLISH, TEXAS WOMEN'S UNIVERSITY

Always be conscious of the fact that people may be at the school for more than an education. Keeping an eye on your stuff and locking your bike securely is not paranoia.

GRADUATE, POLITICAL SCIENCE, UNIVERSITY OF FLORIDA

Use the buddy system. It's always better to walk with a friend than wander by yourself.

SENIOR, POLITICAL SCIENCE, UNIVERSITY OF WASHINGTON

TRENT'S SURVIVAL TIP

Check out *campussafety.org* for information on campus crime news, statistics, and links, as well as sections on legal statutes and congressional acts against campus crime.

Never walk home by yourself at night if you are intoxicated (drunk or high); should something happen, you may not be in the right frame of mind to handle it. And don't let people who have been drinking drive you *anywhere*—just call the shuttle or a cab!

SENIOR, BIOLOGY, OBERLIN COLLEGE

Try not to get so drunk that you are unable to protect yourself, and if you do get that drunk, make sure you are with friends you can trust.

GRADUATE, GOVERNMENT, DARTMOUTH COLLEGE

Never take an open drink from someone you don't know.

SENIOR, POLITICAL SCIENCE, UNIVERSITY OF MASSACHUSETTS—AMHERST

TRUST IS SOMETHING EARNED

A girl should know a guy before she lets him come to her house, and she should always meet him somewhere for the first couple of dates.

SENIOR, JOURNALISM, UNIVERSITY OF TEXAS—AUSTIN

Know your dorm neighbors, so if you see someone who shouldn't be there he will stand out and look suspicious.

SENIOR, POLITICAL SCIENCE, UNIVERSITY OF NORTH TEXAS

"During any given academic year, 2.8 percent of women will experience a completed and/or attempted rape. . . . Almost 60 percent of completed rapes that occurred on campus took place in the victim's residence, 31 percent occurred in other living quarters on campus, and 10.3 percent took place in a fraternity. . . . For both completed and attempted rapes, about 9 in 10 offenders were known to the victim."

Fisher, Bonnie S., Frances T. Cullen, and Michael G. Turner. "The Sexual Victimization of College Women." National Institute of Justice and Bureau of Justice Statistics. December 2000.

Mark your name on EVERYTHING!

GRADUATE, EXERCISE PHYSIOLOGY/MEDICINE, BRIGHAM YOUNG UNIVERSITY

Don't leave your stuff sitting around. As much as you'd like to believe that no one wants your Biochemistry book, you'd be surprised—there are weirdos out there.

GRADUATE, PSYCHOLOGY/ORGANIZATIONAL STUDIES, UNIVERSITY OF MICHIGAN—ANN ARBOR

Don't bring too much expensive stuff—it just gets in the way. Make sure that everything you really care about is secure and that the rest can be replaced easily.

GRADUATE, POLITICAL SCIENCE, UNIVERSITY OF CALIFORNIA—SAN DIEGO

Carry a big backpack. If you have a small backpack you may have to carry some of your books or belongings by hand. If you do that, it will be easier to misplace or lose something. You need to be able to fit everything you need in your bag, because there are no lockers in college.

SENIOR, PSYCHOLOGY/SOCIAL BEHAVIOR, UNIVERSITY OF CALIFORNIA—IRVINE

Keep your stuff *with you* when you are in the library; so many people get their bags stolen.

SENIOR, BIOLOGY, OBERLIN COLLEGE

Buy a laptop lock if you have a laptop. I was the talk of the library because I was one of the few people who owned one, but I started a trend—everyone else started buying one, too.

GRADUATE, POLITICAL SCIENCE, UNIVERSITY OF CALIFORNIA—SAN DIEGO

Buy a trunk or safe box so you can keep money, jewelry, and expensive stuff locked up. **Establish rules with your living buddies about who visits and under what supervision.**

SENIOR, SOCIAL WORK, NIAGARA UNIVERSITY

Bring a padlock with you. Your dorm room should have a closet with a place to use the lock.

GRADUATE, BIOLOGY, UNIVERSITY OF CALIFORNIA—LOS ANGELES

DON'T FLASH THE ICE

Don't boast about your new tech gadgets—that's the most obvious invite for having your stuff stolen.

GRADUATE, SOCIOLOGY, UNIVERSITY OF CALIFORNIA—IRVINE

Don't keep expensive things out in broad daylight.

JUNIOR, BIOLOGY, ARIZONA STATE UNIVERSITY

You will get robbed at least once, whether it's a CD or an entire living room.

GRADUATE, ADVERTISING, MICHIGAN STATE UNIVERSITY

7 DINING DO'S AND DON'TS

Practice eating cardboard to get used to the food in the dining hall.

SENIOR, BIOLOGY, STATE UNIVERSITY OF NEW YORK—UNIVERSITY AT BUFFALO

Never buy a meal plan that doesn't convert its credits/points/meals into dollar value.

GRADUATE, ANTHROPOLOGY, ARIZONA STATE UNIVERSITY

Keep a large supply of Tums on hand at all times.

SENIOR, PSYCHOLOGY, STATE UNIVERSITY OF NEW YORK—UNIVERSITY AT BUFFALO

Although the food might seem good at first, when it is served in such a predictable and unchanging rotation it gets old very quickly.

JUNIOR, COGNITIVE SCIENCE, UNIVERSITY OF VIRGINIA

When you find something that you like, don't eat it all the time—you'll get sick of it!

SENIOR, BIOLOGY, TOWSON UNIVERSITY

I was gonna make sure I was getting my money's worth in the dining hall. I think Dining Services lost money on me—I ate like a horse. I also made friends with some of the ladies behind the counter, and they hooked me up with large portions.

SENIOR, BIOLOGY, COLLEGE OF WILLIAM & MARY

The food was not all that bad, and hey . . . I already paid for it, I might as well eat it.

GRADUATE, PSYCHOLOGY, SYRACUSE UNIVERSITY

IT BEATS COOKING FOR YOURSELF.

GRADUATE, AMERICAN CIVILIZATIONS, BROWN UNIVERSITY

Sixty-six percent of freshmen don't consume the recommended five servings of fruits and vegetables a day. Similarly, 60 percent eat too much artery-clogging saturated fat.

Tufts Longitudinal Health Study. 2002.

WEIGHT WATCHING

I would come to the dining hall, see that the food was bad—but still eat some of it—then go back to my room still hungry and order a pizza or Chinese food. That was not a good idea. I definitely put on the freshman fifteen.

GRADUATE, NEUROSCIENCE AND BEHAVIOR, WESLEYAN UNIVERSITY

Dining hall food is fattening! Eat a balanced meal (yes, including vegetables!) and drink orange juice or milk instead of pop.

SENIOR, PRE-MEDICINE/PSYCHOLOGY, UNIVERSITY OF IOWA

The freshman fifteen can go either way. The food sucked so I lost fifteen pounds!

GRADUATE, BIOLOGY, CLEMSON UNIVERSITY

I quickly learned that I needed to vary my foods: McDonald's three times a week wasn't going to be healthy.

GRADUATE, SOCIOLOGY/FAMILY STUDIES AND HUMAN DEVELOPMENT, UNIVERSITY OF ARIZONA

You *must* monitor your food intake! **They'll let you eat till you pop, and you will!** Be mindful of your eating habits—too many people make themselves miserable because they are not attentive and then they're shocked by their reflection or their parents' reactions at a holiday.

GRADUATE, PSYCHOLOGY/UNIVERSITY SCHOLARS PROGRAM, XAVIER UNIVERSITY

Fifty-nine percent of students say they know their diet is worse since coming to college. Thirty-two percent of all students report a decline in their body image during their freshman year.

Tufts Longitudinal Health Study. 2002.

Load up on hard-boiled eggs to take to your room for when hunger sets in later.

GRADUATE, POLITICAL SCIENCE, FLORIDA INTERNATIONAL UNIVERSITY

It is a good idea to keep some spare snacks in your room for those times when dinner is not edible.

GRADUATE, GOVERNMENT, COLLEGE OF WILLIAM & MARY

Bring Tupperware and "steal" the cereal and fruit and bread. (It's not really stealing, is it? Technically you did *pay* for it . . . right?!)

SENIOR, BIOLOGY, OBERLIN COLLEGE

Take fruits out of the dining hall because **you are going to be hungry late at night.**

GRADUATE, ZOOLOGY, CONNECTICUT COLLEGE

I quickly learned to steer clear of anything with "medley," "hash," or "casserole" in the name; anything "over rice," which usually means "*nasty* over rice"; and meat with gray sauce.

SENIOR, BIOLOGY, OBERLIN COLLEGE

Be very careful of the meat they serve later in the week. Monday's meatloaf has a strange way of reappearing in Friday's spaghetti sauce.

SENIOR, BIOMEDICAL SCIENCES, MARQUETTE UNIVERSITY

Don't eat anything you can't readily identify.

JUNIOR, NEUROSCIENCE, UNIVERSITY OF PITTSBURGH

A BOX OF INSTANT NOODLES IS A MUST!

JUNIOR, BIOLOGY, STATE UNIVERSITY OF NEW YORK—BINGHAMTON UNIVERSITY

Chef Boyardee really knows what he is doing.

GRADUATE, BIOCHEMISTRY/SPANISH, UNIVERSITY OF WISCONSIN—MADISON

Check the school newspaper; there is always something offered for free in terms of food.

SENIOR, ANTHROPOLOGY/INTERNATIONAL STUDIES, NORTHWESTERN UNIVERSITY

I quickly learned how to make my own creations; **it's amazing how much can be done with dining hall food.**

SENIOR, RHETORIC AND COMMUNICATION STUDIES, UNIVERSITY OF RICHMOND

You can make your own pizza bagels with pasta sauce and cheese!

SENIOR, COMMUNICATIONS, UNIVERSITY OF CALIFORNIA—SANTA BARBARA

Quesadillas with spaghetti sauce are delicious.

JUNIOR, PHILOSOPHY, NORTHWESTERN UNIVERSITY

I learned that if you poured clam chowder on top of spaghetti you got seafood fettuccine Alfredo.

GRADUATE, PSYCHOLOGY, UNIVERSITY OF CALIFORNIA—SAN DIEGO

AFTER A SEMESTER OF EATING IN THE DINING HALL, I QUICKLY LEARNED . . .

It's really hard to control yourself when you're offered ice cream 24/7!

SENIOR, CHEMISTRY, CORNELL UNIVERSITY

My mom is an amazing cook.

SENIOR, EXERCISE AND MOVEMENT SCIENCE, UNIVERSITY OF OREGON

The freshman fifteen is directly related to the all-you-can-eat buffet and dessert bar.

GRADUATE, ENGLISH/MUSIC, COLLEGE OF WILLIAM & MARY

What it's like to have food poisoning *nightly*.

GRADUATE, HISTORY, UNIVERSITY OF MASSACHUSETTS

That anything tastes better with salt.

SENIOR, PRE-LAW, UNIVERSITY OF ILLINOIS—URBANA-CHAMPAIGN

8
STAYING FINANCIALLY FIT

Simple. Don't spend what you don't have.

GRADUATE, ENGLISH, MOREHOUSE COLLEGE

MONEY MANAGEMENT

Don't blow your financial aid money on anything but school and books. If you have money left over, save it until the end of the semester when you know you'll get another check for the next semester, and either spend it then or put it in a savings account.

SENIOR, JOURNALISM, UNIVERSITY OF TEXAS—AUSTIN

Have fun, but never at the expense of your necessities. Never leave your bank account empty.

GRADUATE, ENGLISH, GEORGIA STATE UNIVERSITY

Don't charge anything that you couldn't pay for right then and there from your checking account. Keep food money and spending money in two separate accounts.

SENIOR, BIOLOGY, BUCKNELL UNIVERSITY

Sales are good. Look for them. Credit cards are bad. Do not get them. Checking accounts are good. Get one, but don't forget to balance your checkbook.

JUNIOR, PHILOSOPHY, NORTHWESTERN UNIVERSITY

Graduating students have an average of $20,402 in combined education loan and credit card balances.

"Undergraduate Students and Credit Cards: An Analysis of Usage Rates and Trends." Nellie Mae. April 2002.

Keep a twenty-dollar bill in your pocket. It's a lot easier to spend twenty bucks if you have singles and five-dollar bills, but breaking that twenty is a lot harder to do.

GRADUATE, CHEMICAL ENGINEERING, UNIVERSITY OF VIRGINIA

Take out a certain amount of money each week and don't take out any more. If you do that your money will last longer, and you won't keep getting charged all of those ATM fees.

SENIOR, PSYCHOLOGY, HAMPTON UNIVERSITY

Balance your checkbook so that you see how often you are withdrawing money from the ATM. Those $10 withdrawals add up quickly.

JUNIOR, MICROBIOLOGY AND CELL SCIENCE, UNIVERSITY OF FLORIDA

Set a budget for yourself, try to limit extraneous expenses, and **do not hesitate to tell your girlfriend that you can't always buy dinner.**

GRADUATE, POLITICAL SCIENCE, UNIVERSITY OF FLORIDA

Always balance your checkbook and remember that you want to have money left over for Spring Break and Beach Week!

SENIOR, GOVERNMENT, UNIVERSITY OF VIRGINIA

Stick with one guilty pleasure that you can waste money on. CDs, shoes, concerts, what have you . . . but try to discipline yourself to one thing.

GRADUATE, ETHNIC STUDIES/HISTORY, BROWN UNIVERSITY

THE DEVIL IN DISGUISE

Do not get a credit card, no matter how many they toss in your face. Credit cards are the devil in disguise.

SENIOR, JOURNALISM, UNIVERSITY OF TEXAS—AUSTIN

Do not get a credit card. I have never had a credit card and I made it through four years of college just fine. I have so many friends who charged up their credit cards and now have problems paying off the charges and the interest.

GRADUATE, BUSINESS ADMINISTRATION, UNIVERSITY OF MISSOURI—COLUMBIA

Credit-card debt *really* is a big deal! I racked up so much debt and I didn't even realize it. A piece of plastic lets you use more money faster, so be careful with it. Budget your money!

SENIOR, CHEMISTRY, CORNELL UNIVERSITY

Get a credit card and don't use it. Or, if you do, only spend money that you have. It's time to start building credit now. I know people who had to drop out of school to pay off debts.

SENIOR, LINGUISTICS, BRIGHAM YOUNG UNIVERSITY

Pay your credit-card bill off in full every month. If you don't trust yourself not to splurge, use it only for gasoline for your car or something like that. Doing so will build outstanding credit so that when you graduate you can take loans from the bank more easily for "real world" things.

SENIOR, BIOLOGY/ENVIRONMENTAL STUDIES, WASHINGTON COLLEGE

KNOW THE FACTS

In 2002 Impulse Research Corporation surveyed 208 college students over the Internet for the Chubb Group of Insurance Companies and learned that 49 percent of college students receive card applications daily or weekly.

According to the 2002 Financial Services Study conducted by Student Monitor, a research firm that tracks lifestyle trends of college students, 54 percent of college students surveyed owned at least one credit card in their name and 12 percent owned three or more.

Median credit-card debt per student rose from $1,222 in 1998 to $1,770 in 2001, while the proportion of balances from $3,000 to $7,000 rose 61 percent from 14 percent to 21 percent.

"Undergraduate Students and Credit Cards: An Analysis of Usage Rates and Trends." Nellie Mae. April 2002.

Get a part-time job. **You appreciate your money when you can translate a dollar into how long you'd have to work to get it.**

GRADUATE, ENGLISH, CORNELL UNIVERSITY

Find a good summer job and save as much money as you can.

SENIOR, ACCOUNTING, UTAH STATE UNIVERSITY

"About three-quarters of all four-year college students now earn a paycheck, and about one-quarter of them work full time."

Choy, Susan P. "Access & Persistence: Findings from 10 Years of Longitudinal Research on Students." American Council on Education. 2002.

ONCE UPON A CAMPUS

SCHOLARLY AID

Check the Internet for scholarships; there are a lot out there.

GRADUATE, ZOOLOGY, CONNECTICUT COLLEGE

Scholarships are definitely the way to go; one would be surprised at how much money there is for students that's just waiting to be asked for.

GRADUATE, ENGLISH, UNIVERSITY OF FLORIDA

Try to get scholarships—there is one for everybody. *In fact, Joe Smith from Yourtown, USA, can probably find a specialized scholarship, such as one for a trumpet player interested in attending Beefcake College.*

GRADUATE, PSYCHOLOGY, EAST TENNESSEE STATE UNIVERSITY

There is always free food around. Go to meetings that offer free dinner or treats.

GRADUATE, MATH, CARLETON COLLEGE

Buy food and make it whenever you can. **Make a big meal on Sunday and eat leftovers.** Get a membership at a Sam's Club or Costco.

SENIOR, GOVERNMENT, UNIVERSITY OF VIRGINIA

Always eat on your meal plan unless it's a special occasion.

SENIOR, ENGLISH/PSYCHOLOGY, UNIVERSITY OF MICHIGAN—ANN ARBOR

Wendy's is known for their 99-cent menu and it will become one of your best friends. You can make at least three meals out of ten dollars.

GRADUATE, BUSINESS ADMINISTRATION, FLORIDA AGRICULTURAL AND MECHANICAL UNIVERSITY

Learn how to cook! It can be a good way to get your mind off of things and save money. It is also a lot healthier than eating out. Invite friends over and offer to cook in exchange for them doing the clean-up.

GRADUATE, BIOCHEMISTRY, UNIVERSITY OF CALIFORNIA—DAVIS

Shop consignment! Learn about all the free perks on campus and the cheap discounts you get as a student. Most airlines, restaurants, etc., offer a discount to college students if you show an ID.

SENIOR, JOURNALISM, UNIVERSITY OF TEXAS—AUSTIN

Shop at the dollar store, garage sales, eBay, and bulk discount stores like Costco and Food 4 Less.

SENIOR, LINGUISTICS, BRIGHAM YOUNG UNIVERSITY

CLIP COUPONS AND FIND FREE THINGS TO DO WITH FRIENDS.

SENIOR, BIOLOGY, BUCKNELL UNIVERSITY

Share books with friends in your classes. For fast cash, do the psychology experiments you see advertised.

GRADUATE, ETHNIC STUDIES/HISTORY, BROWN UNIVERSITY

Live off of ramen noodles, the ultimate cheap college feast.

GRADUATE, PSYCHOLOGY, EAST TENNESSEE STATE UNIVERSITY

Shop around when buying books (save your receipts). Try to stall laundry until your next trip home.

JUNIOR, BIOLOGY, UNIVERSITY OF MICHIGAN—ANN ARBOR

You'd be amazed at what you can find by asking around in your dorm instead of going out and buying it (i.e., printer paper, even some furniture!).

JUNIOR, SCIENCE PRE-PROFESSIONAL, UNIVERSITY OF NOTRE DAME

MANAGING YOUR FINANCES

Trent Says:

If you're going to have a credit card, tell the credit-card company that you want a $1,000 limit. And don't use it. Because if you don't live like a student while you're a student, you will wind up living like a student when you graduate. Suddenly you're going to have debt payments—not just on the consumer debt, but on your student loans as well.

Don't buy a bunch of new stuff before you go to college. You don't know what you need, you don't know what the fashion is going to be, so you'll just end up throwing money away.

Seppy Says:

Stay away from the people with the little tables and the credit cards and free gifts. *Stay away*. If your school sponsors a class for freshmen on credit cards and debt in general, take it. Many people have no clue just how much debt they can build up. You just don't want to go there.

If you use student-loan money for junk food, that junk food becomes exceptionally expensive over time. The interest you will be paying on your loans adds a gross amount to every dollar you borrow. So, just because you're getting the money and it seems sort of free and easy, it's not so free and easy.

9
THE NEW SOCIAL YOU

Walk around with a big Mexican hat on. People will notice.

SENIOR, LINGUISTICS, BRIGHAM YOUNG UNIVERSITY

The best way to meet people in college is to get involved! And when I say get involved, that means in anything. If you like to dance, go join the dance team. If you like to swim, go to the pool. Only in college will you find so many young people in one place who all want to meet people. There are others just like you out there on campus . . . looking to meet people! And I can tell you this: They would most likely value your friendship just as much as you would value theirs. **GET INVOLVED.**

GRADUATE, BIOLOGY/NUTRITION, PENNSYLVANIA STATE UNIVERSITY

Find an activity you're interested in and go participate in it. It doesn't matter if it's academic, athletic, or something else. If the activity interests you, you'll likely find people who interest you there.

GRADUATE, INFORMATICS, UNIVERSITY OF WASHINGTON

Attend events that support issues you are adamant about—it's the best way to find people who share the same interests as you.

GRADUATE, POLITICAL ECONOMY OF INDUSTRIAL SOCIETIES, UNIVERSITY OF CALIFORNIA—BERKELEY

Some of the best friends you'll ever make are the least obvious to you.

SENIOR, MICROBIOLOGY AND CELL SCIENCE, UNIVERSITY OF FLORIDA

The first few weeks of school are the time to go to the parties that you normally wouldn't go to. . . . That's when everyone goes. Meet people that way; then you can settle in to your own little niche.

GRADUATE, CHEMICAL ENGINEERING, UNIVERSITY OF VIRGINIA

Meet the people around you in your first year. After that it keeps getting harder because everyone is already associated with another group of friends.

GRADUATE, BIOLOGY/ENGLISH, INDIANA UNIVERSITY—BLOOMINGTON

GO GREEK! Hey, I did it!

JUNIOR, CHEMICAL BIOLOGY, STEVENS INSTITUTE OF TECHNOLOGY

In actuality I never imagined joining a fraternity, but once I met the other guys there we all clicked and it made sense because I hung out with them a great deal anyway. It is cheesy, but it truly made my college experience.

GRADUATE, INTERNATIONAL STUDIES/RUSSIAN, JOHNS HOPKINS UNIVERSITY

My most memorable experiences were just hanging out in my fraternity house with all my friends. Spring Break in Amsterdam with nine of my fraternity brothers was one of the greatest times of my life.

GRADUATE, ECONOMICS/PHILOSOPHY, STATE UNIVERSITY OF NEW YORK—BINGHAMTON UNIVERSITY

I just said "hi," and tried to talk to as many people as I could—even if it was just small talk—for the first couple of days, especially people in my dorm or classes. Eventually, you discover who you really enjoy talking to and will start hanging out with them.

GRADUATE, SOCIOLOGY, UNIVERSITY OF HAWAII—MANOA

I met people by talking to anyone and everyone who I found remotely interesting in any of my classes. It may be difficult to do at first, and some of the people you approach may not take to it well, but in the long run it definitely pays a greater dividend than do clubs/groups.

GRADUATE, PSYCHOLOGY/UNIVERSITY SCHOLARS PROGRAM, XAVIER UNIVERSITY

Meet as many new people as you can! You never know where you'll find your new best friend.

SENIOR, BIOCHEMISTRY/MOLECULAR BIOLOGY, CORNELL UNIVERSITY

READY-MADE FRIENDS

Network. Use people you meet in class and your dorm to meet people they know—try not to pass up the opportunity to go out with a new group of people.

SENIOR, ANTHROPOLOGY, UNIVERSITY OF TORONTO

WHEN ALL ELSE FAILS . . .

Visit all the rooms in your dorm or join a club for fun. If this doesn't work, start baking cookies really fast. Then they will come to you.

SENIOR, MARKETING, UNIVERSITY OF NOTRE DAME

Sit next to people you think are interesting and strike up a conversation about the class.

SENIOR, PSYCHOLOGY, FLORIDA ATLANTIC UNIVERSITY

BE OUTGOING: Be the first one to talk when the TA asks you to break into groups. It's easy to stay outgoing when you start out that way, but when you start out quiet, it's tough to switch roles.

GRADUATE, POLITICAL SCIENCE/SOCIOLOGY/LEGAL STUDIES, UNIVERSITY OF WISCONSIN—MADISON

Always be the person in class that anyone can ask for help in that particular subject, and you will automatically become popular. Knowledge draws popularity.

GRADUATE, ENGLISH, MOREHOUSE COLLEGE

SEPPY'S SURVIVAL TIP

Meet people in the dining hall by table-hopping. There were whole ends of dining halls that I never sat in until my junior year of college—a total waste of time. I could have met so many more great people if I had table-hopped from the get-go.

Talk! People are like animals—if you leave them alone, they'll leave you alone.

GRADUATE, PHYSICS, GROSSMONT COLLEGE; SENIOR, INTERDISCIPLINARY STUDIES IN PHYSICS/BIOLOGY/PSYCHOLOGY, SAN DIEGO STATE UNIVERSITY

Find people sitting alone in the dining hall, and, after introducing yourself, sit down to eat with them.

GRADUATE, ENGLISH, CORNELL UNIVERSITY

Be outgoing and smile—don't be afraid to reach out and put yourself out there.

SENIOR, PSYCHOLOGY, UNIVERSITY OF MICHIGAN

She crawled into a box at a party.

GRADUATE, CRIMINAL JUSTICE/POLITICAL SCIENCE/HISTORY, INDIANA UNIVERSITY—BLOOMINGTON

I started looking at my other friendships more critically. Once you have a really true friend, your standards for friendship rise.

GRADUATE, INTERNATIONAL RELATIONS, BROWN UNIVERSITY

I punched her. We met in our self-defense (Hankido) class.

GRADUATE, POLITICAL ECONOMY OF INDUSTRIAL SOCIETIES, UNIVERSITY OF CALIFORNIA—BERKELEY

I bailed him out of jail.

SENIOR, ENGLISH, ROLLINS COLLEGE AND FLORIDA STATE UNIVERSITY

10

RED IN THE FACE

College is nothing but a list of embarrassing experiences.
Get ready to enjoy them all

SENIOR, POLITICAL SCIENCE, INDIANA UNIVERSITY

A "CLOTHES" ENCOUNTER

Let's just say I LOST MY SHORTS.

SENIOR, ECONOMICS, UNIVERSITY OF NEVADA—LAS VEGAS

My most embarrassing moment was coming home on New Year's Eve and having my roommate inform me that my new shiny silver pants had a huge rip in the butt. I had been out all night like that!

SENIOR, PRE-LAW, UNIVERSITY OF ILLINOIS—URBANA-CHAMPAIGN

I got caught streaking the Lawn by a police officer . . . he let me go, though.

SENIOR, PSYCHOLOGY, UNIVERSITY OF VIRGINIA

For crew initiation I had to wear the same outfit for a whole week and then sing and dance in the cafeteria!

GRADUATE, BIOLOGY, GEORGETOWN UNIVERSITY

AN ACCIDENTAL AUDIENCE

I slipped on the ice on the sidewalk in front of about 200 people, all gathered together because they knew about the ice patch and were waiting for people to slip.

SENIOR, LINGUISTICS, BRIGHAM YOUNG UNIVERSITY

One night at a party, some friends convinced a girl I had never laid eyes on before that I was in love with her. Needless to say, when she confronted me about it in front of a bunch of people, **I wanted to crawl into a hole.**

GRADUATE, HISTORY, UNIVERSITY OF MASSACHUSETTS

I was showing a group of students and their parents around campus and I slipped and fell down a massive flight of wet stairs. Afterward, I triumphantly got up and yelled "I'M OKAY!" Nevertheless, it was embarrassing.

SENIOR, GENDER STUDIES/RELIGIOUS STUDIES, BROWN UNIVERSITY

I accidentally pulled out a plug in a public computer room and every computer was shut down . . . it happened before final exams, when papers are due!

SENIOR, BIOLOGY, STATE UNIVERSITY OF NEW YORK—UNIVERSITY AT BUFFALO

My freshman year, I was at a party during the winter and tripped headlong into a swimming pool. Mind you, I was sober.

SENIOR, GOVERNMENT, UNIVERSITY OF TEXAS—AUSTIN

I passed out during a fire drill and had to be carried upstairs when it was over.

SENIOR, NEUROSCIENCE, UNIVERSITY OF ROCHESTER

My most embarrassing moment was when I realized how thin the walls were in the dorms and that everyone could hear me singing in my room.

GRADUATE, BIOCHEMISTRY/SPANISH, UNIVERSITY OF WISCONSIN—MADISON

First day of classes. Freshman year. A seventy-five-person lecture. I tipped over in my desk as I was reaching for my pen. Everyone, including the professor, laughed at me.

GRADUATE, CHEMICAL ENGINEERING, UNIVERSITY OF VIRGINIA

The lab gloves in my Basic Chemistry class were slippery and I dropped a bottle, sending a very strong base flying everywhere. They called the fire department and made me stand in the chemical shower in the middle of class! When they finally took me to the ER, they said I was fine and released me. But I made that evening's news!

SENIOR, EVOLUTION/ECOLOGY, UNIVERSITY OF CALIFORNIA—DAVIS

I meant to send a romantic e-mail to my boyfriend and accidentally sent it to a professor instead. (The professor's e-mail address was listed underneath my boyfriend's in my e-mail address book.) I got an A in the class!

GRADUATE, HISTORY, RUTGERS—THE STATE UNIVERSITY OF NEW JERSEY

I had to leave freshman camp early because I had an allergic reaction after I sat in a pile of fire ants.

JUNIOR, BIOLOGY/CHEMISTRY, HOUSTON BAPTIST UNIVERSITY

When I got to college my freshman year I didn't know how to do my own laundry. I spent a month washing my clothes in fabric softener. What did I know? Now I know better.

SENIOR, ENGLISH/CREATIVE WRITING AND FILM/PHOTOGRAPHY, HOLLINS UNIVERSITY

A BIRD POOPED ON MY LEG DURING ORIENTATION WEEK. **It was the first time I had met anyone from the school and for the rest of the week everyone knew me as the girl the bird pooped on.**

JUNIOR, BIOMEDICAL ENGINEERING, SAINT LOUIS UNIVERSITY

I fell asleep in my friends' room, and they put a large plastic rooster head in bed next to me and took a large color photo.

GRADUATE, ENGLISH/FRENCH, CORNELL UNIVERSITY

I walked in on my roommate not once, not twice, but three times when she was mostly naked with her boyfriend. She didn't have a signal system.

SENIOR, BIOCHEMISTRY/ENGLISH, UNIVERSITY OF CALIFORNIA—DAVIS

Sometimes you just gotta take it and not be embarrassed. It makes life a lot easier.

GRADUATE, PHYSICS, GROSSMONT COLLEGE; SENIOR, INTERDISCIPLINARY STUDIES IN PHYSICS/BIOLOGY/PSYCHOLOGY, SAN DIEGO STATE UNIVERSITY

Hey, it's college. Nothing is embarrassing.

GRADUATE, BIOLOGY, SPRING HILL COLLEGE

11

ON THE SIDE

Being involved makes you feel like you're really a part of the university, not just another nameless student.

JUNIOR, BIOLOGY/CHEMISTRY, HOUSTON BAPTIST UNIVERSITY

College is not the time to be a wallflower. Check the bulletin boards for a club or an event where you can meet others with similar interests. One of my biggest regrets is not taking advantage of all the different activities that only college campuses have to offer.

GRADUATE, ENGLISH/FRENCH, CORNELL UNIVERSITY

Choir, student honor council, hosting receptions, business fraternity, church groups, work. **BEING A STUDENT IS ONLY PART OF MY LIFE—I HAVE TO DO OTHER THINGS TO KEEP MYSELF BALANCED AND TO MAINTAIN MY PERSPECTIVE.**

SENIOR, BUSINESS ADMINISTRATION, ROANOKE COLLEGE

I suggest going to as many different meetings as possible. Even if you're only remotely interested in the club, they might present something that will convince you it's worth your time.

GRADUATE, SOCIOLOGY, UNIVERSITY OF CALIFORNIA—IRVINE

I participate in student government, band, a social club (i.e., fraternity), a community service organization, and Philiatros, a pre-health professional organization. My rationale is that I will never again in my life have the opportunity to do so many varied things or, in the case of band, have access to the kinds of resources that a university offers. Take advantage.

SENIOR, BIOLOGY/VOCATIONAL MINISTRY, OKLAHOMA CHRISTIAN UNIVERSITY

BE ALL YOU CAN BE

I organized free backpacking, ice climbing, horseback riding, kayaking, skiing and snowboarding trips, and art tours for fellow students through a grant given to the college. I loved to make people focus on things other than school by throwing wonderful trips at them.

GRADUATE, BIOCHEMISTRY/MOLECULAR BIOLOGY, REED COLLEGE

I participated in the ballroom dance club, kickboxing, and Supplemental Instruction, and I tutored. **I WANTED TO KEEP A BALANCE BETWEEN MY ACADEMIC INTERESTS AND MY PHYSICAL FITNESS.** *I was also very active in the pre-law fraternity at my school, which became very important to me down the road.*

GRADUATE, PSYCHOLOGY, UNIVERSITY OF TEXAS—AUSTIN

participated in student government. I really like to argue and I also wanted to get involved, so Student Senate sounded great. After two years as a senator, I eventually became my university's student body president. **IT WILL BE A WHILE BEFORE I GET TO BE THE CEO OF A HALF-A-MILLION-DOLLAR-A-YEAR ORGANIZATION AGAIN.**

SENIOR, BIOLOGY/CHEMISTRY, SEATTLE PACIFIC UNIVERSITY

I founded the Free Burma Coalition at my school. I was shocked that I knew so little about the situation in Myanmar and was tired of how the Free Tibet campaign became so commercialized. By working on this cause independently, I felt I was doing something more worthwhile. I also taught spinning classes (aerobic exercise, not deejaying) to keep in shape and earn some money on the side. Finally, I worked at the radio station—I thought it was an excellent and educational way to have fun. Plus, I was exposed to more of the "real world" when doing promotions away from campus.

GRADUATE, INTERNATIONAL RELATIONS, BROWN UNIVERSITY

ACADEMIC ASPIRATIONS

I am involved in a lot of organizations related to engineering. I participate in these organizations because most of my time is spent with my classmates and with doing work related to our major. Being in organizations that are related to my major gives me a voice in what happens within the school and my department.

JUNIOR, BIOMEDICAL ENGINEERING/PRE-MEDICINE, SAINT LOUIS UNIVERSITY

I'm a Political Science major and I plan on going to law school. I joined academic clubs like the Pre-Law Society early and knew more about applying to law school as a second-year than graduating seniors.

SENIOR, POLITICAL SCIENCE/CHINESE LANGUAGE, UNIVERSITY OF CALIFORNIA—IRVINE

TRENT'S SURVIVAL TIP

Choose one thing and try it. You can always change your mind. It gets you out, and it helps you schedule and balance the things that are going on in your life.

I'm not a big advocate of joining lots of different clubs. If you really are genuinely interested in being a member of three clubs, great, but don't do it just because you think more is better.

Playing intramural sports is great because you do just as much socializing as you do practicing—it's much more low-key than playing a varsity sport but you still have a great time and get exercise.

SENIOR, MATHEMATICAL ECONOMICS, COLGATE UNIVERSITY

I became secretary of the Outdoor Adventure Club and now I hang out with active people. We have gone kayaking, white-water rafting, and rock climbing together, and we have a blast. **YOU HAVE TO JOIN CLUBS AND ORGANIZATIONS THAT GENUINELY INTEREST YOU, NOT JUST BECAUSE THEY HAPPEN TO BE WHAT EVERYONE ELSE IS DOING.**

SENIOR, BIOLOGY, MILLSAPS COLLEGE

My most memorable experience was being on the baseball field every day, knowing I was working harder and doing more than the typical college student, and being part of a great group of guys.

GRADUATE, POLITICAL SCIENCE, UNIVERSITY OF THE SOUTH

*I pledged a sorority and **it was the best thing I did throughout my college career.** It opened so many doors and introduced me to my very best friends. I would recommend it to anyone.*

GRADUATE, MASS COMMUNICATIONS, NORTHEASTERN STATE UNIVERSITY

I was a member of a fraternity—it gave me an opportunity to run an organization with a bunch of guys I felt really comfortable with.

SENIOR, JOURNALISM/PHILOSOPHY, SYRACUSE UNIVERSITY

In a Harvard School of Public Health survey of 119 four-year schools in 2001, 75 percent of students who lived in frats were binge drinkers, compared to 35 percent of those who lived in substance-free dorms.

Wechsler, Henry, et al. "Trends in College Binge Drinking During a Period of Increased Prevention Efforts: Findings from Four Harvard School of Public Health College Alcohol Study Surveys: 1993-2001." *Journal of American College Health.* March 2002.

ON THE SIDE

I was in a business fraternity. I joined at first for networking, but I made so many new friends and participated in so many activities.

GRADUATE, BUSINESS ADMINISTRATION, UNIVERSITY OF MISSOURI—COLUMBIA

I was in a sorority because it was a good way to get involved, both socially and within the community. Also, networking with alumni to find a job was important!

SENIOR, ANTHROPOLOGY/INTERNATIONAL STUDIES, NORTHWESTERN UNIVERSITY

I joined a social sorority, but make sure it is right for you before you join one.

GRADUATE, ENGLISH, TEXAS WOMEN'S UNIVERSITY

I am in a sorority because I love that I feel like I'm at camp when I'm really at school!

SENIOR, PSYCHOLOGY, UNIVERSITY OF MICHIGAN

Seppy Says:

At big schools, pledging a fraternity or sorority can be incredibly important. Having an affinity at a big school is necessary, and Greek life is one way to do that. Being in these organizations can also help when you're looking for old exams to study from or for advice from upperclassmen about classes and professors.

In some cases, though, it's so hard to get in to frats and sororities. Take a really deep breath. At the end of the day, if you've developed intimate and close relationships with a bunch of guys or girls, you'll have them as friends whether or not you end up joining the organization.

Trent Says:

I would encourage you not to rush a fraternity or sorority as a freshman. How can you possibly say, "I want to be a member of this organization for four years" based on one week of interaction with them?

I don't think fraternities and sororities are good or bad; I just think they are. I'm a real advocate of waiting to join one until you have a better sense of who's in them, what they're about, and whether they're a good fit for you.

I have been a mentor for inner-city African American males and a member of Noon Run, an organization that makes and serves lunch to the homeless. I wanted to take advantage of the diverse culture that Milwaukee offers and interact with people that I normally would never meet.

SENIOR, BIOMEDICAL SCIENCES, MARQUETTE UNIVERSITY

I participated in many identity groups, such as the Women of Color Collective and Ujamaa, a group for African American students. I think it's important for minority students to form support groups, especially during college. There are still a lot of issues that the disabled, homosexual, and students of color have to face that are not understood by the majority.

GRADUATE, NEUROSCIENCE AND BEHAVIOR, WESLEYAN UNIVERSITY

I worked as a peer counselor for victims of sexual assault, which was a problem on our campus.

GRADUATE, GOVERNMENT, DARTMOUTH COLLEGE

I VOLUNTEERED AT THE HEALTH CLINIC TO SEE IF I REALLY WANTED TO BE PRE-MED.

SENIOR, CHEMISTRY, CORNELL UNIVERSITY

I played soccer with Special Olympic athletes for two fall semesters as a community service project connected to my school. I did that since I knew it would be fun and because it was something I'd never tried before. Playing soccer for SO was probably the most fun experience I've had in college.

SENIOR, HEALTH ADMINISTRATION AND POLICY, UNIVERSITY OF MARYLAND—BALTIMORE COUNTY

I am involved in a national service fraternity. This is important to me because I feel it is not only personally fulfilling to do community service, but also because it benefits others.

JUNIOR, BIOMEDICAL ENGINEERING/PRE-MEDICINE, SAINT LOUIS UNIVERSITY

ON THE SIDE

12 YOU'RE NOT IN KANSAS ANYMORE

Forget everything you know and everything you learned in high school. Forget your study habits and forget how you learned to write papers. It's all gonna change, and you'd better be ready for it.

SENIOR, LINGUISTICS, BRIGHAM YOUNG UNIVERSITY

You can cram and slide your way through high school, but it is difficult to do that—and do well—in college. **FORCE YOURSELF TO BE DISCIPLINED AND DILIGENT.** It will pay off.

GRADUATE, ENGLISH/FRENCH, CORNELL UNIVERSITY

If you flew through high school, get ready. Learn how to study if you have never done it before. Practice writing analytically, not just writing about how you feel. There's a big difference!

SENIOR, BIOLOGY/CHEMISTRY, DENISON UNIVERSITY

HIGH SCHOOL IS NOTHING LIKE COLLEGE. YOU ACTUALLY HAVE TO MAKE AN EFFORT IN COLLEGE.

GRADUATE, BIOLOGY, CLEMSON UNIVERSITY

You will spend a lot more time doing homework in college. Many teachers believe that their class is your only class.

GRADUATE, PSYCHOLOGY/BIOLOGY, SAINT LOUIS UNIVERSITY

THERE IS NO FORMULA FOR SUCCESS. During freshman year you'll spend a lot of time finding out about yourself along with expanding your academic capabilities. Don't be afraid of the big bad college. Everyone thinks college is going to be so hard, but if you take the first few weeks to feel things out, you will be fine.

SENIOR, GENDER STUDIES/RELIGIOUS STUDIES, BROWN UNIVERSITY

For the first time in your life it's your responsibility to make sure your work gets done. **MOM AND DAD AREN'T THERE TO WATCH OVER YOUR SHOULDER.** *If you don't do your work, you'll fail—so do it for yourself. Anyway, it feels better doing it for yourself than for your parents.*

GRADUATE, BIOMETRY AND STATISTICS, CORNELL UNIVERSITY

PLACING OUT OF COURSES

Trent Says:

If you're going to be a social sciences or humanities major, go ahead and place out of Calculus. The classes that you should not try to get out of are the freshman writing courses. My experience is that no matter what score a student gets on her AP or how good she thinks she was in high school, most high school students do not write well at the college level and they benefit greatly from a college writing class.

Seppy Says:

If you go to a large state school where money is an issue, placing out of courses is a great option. At a smaller school, where freshman English is a twenty-person seminar with writing assignments once a week, that is not a course you want to miss. Learning how to write well early on will be an invaluable asset in all your college classes. If freshman English is a large literature survey based off your AP English Literature class, go ahead and skip it. Since you've already learned the material, I'd rather see you getting into the stuff you're interested in.

College is no more difficult than high school, except that now you are battling a thousand distractions.

GRADUATE, PSYCHOLOGY, NEW YORK UNIVERSITY

Know the syllabus backward and forward so that you know when you need to focus hard on school and when you can relax.

SENIOR, HUMAN DEVELOPMENT AND FAMILY STUDIES, TEXAS TECH UNIVERSITY

You don't learn from the books you are reading, you learn from the application of that knowledge. High school tests often quizzed memorization skills. That's a handy talent to have, but unless you can apply the knowledge you are learning, the whole process is a waste.

GRADUATE, POLITICAL SCIENCE, SAINT JOSEPH'S UNIVERSITY

The core curriculum in college is really designed to help you make a smooth transition from high school. However, just like the transition from junior high to high school, you have to get into a groove. Until you do, look for support from other students—perhaps sophomores and juniors—and DON'T BE AFRAID TO ASK FOR HELP.

GRADUATE, PSYCHOLOGY, COLBY-SAWYER COLLEGE

There is a lot more independent work involved with college. If you can study independently and learn from a book, you will have a great advantage.

GRADUATE, MATH, CARLETON COLLEGE

High school teachers teach you everything you need to know. **COLLEGE PROFESSORS ASSUME YOU'RE GOING TO TEACH YOURSELF.**

GRADUATE, CHEMICAL ENGINEERING, UNIVERSITY OF VIRGINIA

13

HIT THE GROUND RUNNING

You know those "study skills" they always talked about when we were younger? Imagine this—they're actually important!

GRADUATE, ART AND DESIGN, LAGRANGE COLLEGE

READ, READ, READ and don't stop . . .

SENIOR, PSYCHOLOGY, UNIVERSITY AT BUFFALO

Keep up with your work from the beginning. **Study *every* night.**

GRADUATE, POLITICAL SCIENCE, LOUISIANA STATE UNIVERSITY

Don't let things slide—you can't make up an entire semester's worth of work the night before a final.

SENIOR, JOURNALISM/PHILOSOPHY, SYRACUSE UNIVERSITY

Professors love to speak, so be ready to take lots of notes. If you are lucky, some professors will give you study guides as to what will be covered on the exam. Nevertheless, you must go to class, because the best way to understand the material is to be there in person, and it also gives you an opportunity to ask the professor or a fellow student a question.

SENIOR, ACCOUNTING, ST. MARY'S UNIVERSITY (SAN ANTONIO)

Tutors are *great*. Get them—and don't be embarrassed. **In college the smart kids find tutors.**

SENIOR, BIOCHEMISTRY AND MOLECULAR BIOLOGY, CORNELL UNIVERSITY

My number one rule for myself is to go to class. No matter what. If I go to class consistently and take good notes, tests will be doable. No matter how little I read the texts, or even studied, if I went to class I at least got a passing grade.

SENIOR, HISTORY, LOYOLA MARYMOUNT UNIVERSITY

GO TO CLASS. Going to the lectures will let you know exactly what information is important. If you don't go to class, you are on your own. I also recommend re-copying your lecture notes. I was given this tip at college orientation and it worked for me.

GRADUATE, ECONOMICS/GOVERNMENT AND POLITICS, UNIVERSITY OF MARYLAND—COLLEGE PARK

ASK FOR HELP AND GET IT WHEN YOU NEED IT—AND EVEN IF YOU THINK YOU DON'T.

SENIOR, JOURNALISM, UNIVERSITY OF TEXAS—AUSTIN

Remember, there *is* enough time in the day if you use every minute wisely!

SENIOR, ORGANIZATIONAL LEADERSHIP, WEST VIRGINIA UNIVERSITY

You cannot leave anything till the last minute. For tests, begin reviewing a few days in advance. For papers, the amount of time depends on the length of the paper, but leave yourself enough time to do a good outline, rough draft, and final version.

GRADUATE, GOVERNMENT, DARTMOUTH COLLEGE

Figure out what works best for you in terms of time management. Do you write better under pressure or do you like to have a lot of time to revise? Do you want to talk to professors to get advice?

GRADUATE, ANTHROPOLOGY/INTERNATIONAL STUDIES, NORTHWESTERN UNIVERSITY

Treat homework and school like a job and treat your social life like a social life—and try not to mix the two.

It's going to seem like you have a lot of free time because you are only in class for three to four hours a day. When midterms come around, however, you will realize what you were supposed to be doing during that "free time."

GRADUATE, BIOLOGY, COLLEGE OF CHARLESTON

It's really not all that hard to balance work and play. **JUST DO YOUR WORK BEFORE YOU PLAY, AND IF YOU DON'T GET IT DONE, THEN YOU CAN'T PLAY!** Your GPA might be your saving grace someday when applying to law school, med school, or grad school. You might have an average LSAT score, but an amazing GPA speaks loud and clear about what a hard worker and talented student you really are.

SENIOR, GOVERNMENT, LAFAYETTE COLLEGE

always find it helpful to have a calendar and write down when everything is due. That way you're not waiting until the last minute to finish assignments, especially when you have multiple assignments due on one day or in one week.

GRADUATE, NEAR EASTERN AND JUDAIC STUDIES, BRANDEIS UNIVERSITY

Make a schedule and stick to it. It was not until my senior year when I had a full course load, GREs, grad school applications, and a senior thesis to write, all in one semester, that I really learned how helpful this can be. You get enough done and you keep moving rather than getting bogged down and overwhelmed.

GRADUATE, SOCIOLOGY, MILLS COLLEGE

You should expect to **SPEND THE SAME AMOUNT OF TIME STUDYING AS YOU SPEND IN CLASS.** *And don't think that weekends are for hanging around; they are for studying during the day and having fun at night!*

SENIOR, GOVERNMENT, UNIVERSITY OF VIRGINIA

Work hard, play hard: Buckle down and do the work because it will make your time off that much more fun.

SENIOR, PSYCHOLOGY, UNIVERSITY OF VIRGINIA

Seppy Says:

It's crucial to know the Dean of Student Life or Academic Affairs and his assistant. They can often tip you off to campus job opportunities and to what's happening on campus.

Get to know the department secretaries in the departments that interest you. They can give you the inside scoop on what's going on in the department and help you set up appointments with hard-to-reach professors.

It's vital to have a key faculty champion for yourself. Find a professor whose field of study you're interested in or who is really high energy.

Introduce yourself to the folks in the career services office early on. It's a great place to try and look for a part-time job as a freshman. By the time you're a senior they'll know you and like you. Not that they won't help every student, but they'll help you more if they know you.

Trent Says:

Who you should get to know depends on your goals. If you think there's a chance you're going to go to graduate school, making academic contacts early becomes important, especially when the time comes for you to get recommendations. If you're going to be part of a smaller college, the college of arts, for example, then it's important to get to know the administrators in the Registrar's office. Having a contact there might come in handy if you have a problem with your course schedule.

For any office that you're working with, get to know the support staff, not just the head honchos, because the chance of you actually getting through to the dean, or whoever else is in charge, is pretty slim. But if you know the secretary or coordinator, you can often get a lot done in any department.

14

GUILTY PLEASURES

I am procrastination. I never procrastinated until I was in college, but, boy, if you could see me now. Watching TV, chatting with my friends, using AOL Instant Messenger, talking on the phone, napping, surfing the Internet . . .

SENIOR, BIOLOGY/ENVIRONMENTAL STUDIES, WASHINGTON COLLEGE

MY FAVORITE FORM OF PROCRASTINATION WAS . . .

Sleeping and watching *Great Chefs of the World* on the Discovery Channel.

GRADUATE, ENGINEERING SCIENCES, DARTMOUTH COLLEGE

Cooking and looking up professors in search engines to find dirt on them.

SENIOR, BIOLOGY/NEUROSCIENCE/PSYCHOLOGY, BRANDEIS UNIVERSITY

Cleaning. Oddly enough, my favorite time to clean was when I had big assignments due.

GRADUATE, PUBLIC RELATIONS, UNIVERSITY OF GEORGIA

Exercising . . . it kept off the freshman fifteen.

GRADUATE, BIOLOGICAL SCIENCES, SOUTHERN ILLINOIS UNIVERSITY—EDWARDSVILLE

Having water fights in the hall, watching the *Wedding Story* on TLC, having popcorn kernel spitting contests, playing in the snow, and, of course, sleeping!

GRADUATE, BIOLOGY, MIDLAND LUTHERAN COLLEGE

Going to the coffee house for a cup of coffee and chatting with friends, or playing guitar and writing songs with my friends.

SENIOR, MUSIC/ECONOMICS, LAKE FOREST COLLEGE

SNOOD! *All of my friends were addicted to this computer game.*

GRADUATE, ENGLISH/MUSIC, COLLEGE OF WILLIAM & MARY

Surfing the net, going out, hanging out with friends. Heck, I even go to the library just to socialize because there are so many people there I know!!

SENIOR, POLITICAL SCIENCE, UNIVERSITY OF NORTH FLORIDA

I took long walks through the safe neighborhoods around campus. You get to dabble in the old family-centered life you miss; you get exercise and don't end up gorging yourself on pizza with the other kids who'll hate themselves in three months when they realize it added twenty pounds to their frames; and you get to free your mind from the worries that surround you when you're on campus.

GRADUATE, PSYCHOLOGY/UNIVERSITY SCHOLARS PROGRAM, XAVIER UNIVERSITY

I loved to lie around in the grass under a tree on a nice sunny day and just relax! It's the best to get your mind off of those challenging assignments that lie ahead.

SENIOR, PSYCHOLOGY, UNIVERSITY OF MARYLAND—COLLEGE PARK

134

TRENT'S SURVIVAL TIP

No TV in your room! And beware of the Internet; it's the new device of choice for procrastinators nationwide.

THE TELEVISION IS A CURSE!

SENIOR, SOCIAL WORK, NIAGARA UNIVERSITY

Soap operas have really become addictive. I even went so far as to plan one semester so no classes would interfere with my favorite soap!

SENIOR, LEGAL STUDIES, QUINNIPIAC UNIVERSITY

Nintendo. SAVING THE WORLD PLAYING BOND IS INSTANT GRATIFICATION.

GRADUATE, MICROBIOLOGY, INDIANA UNIVERSITY

E-MAIL, E-MAIL, E-MAIL. I don't know how many times I would check it. AOL Instant Messenger was another downfall.

JUNIOR, MICROBIOLOGY AND CELL SCIENCE, UNIVERSITY OF FLORIDA

Using Instant Messenger to keep track of friends was a great way to put off writing a paper. There was also the tendency for "short" breaks to quickly become long, extended chat sessions with friends.

GRADUATE, BIOCHEMISTRY, UNIVERSITY OF CALIFORNIA—DAVIS

The computer—instant messaging, online games, e-mailing. Very addictive!

SENIOR, PSYCHOLOGY, UNIVERSITY OF MISSOURI—KANSAS CITY

GUILTY PLEASURES

136

A research study at Rutgers University revealed that students who reported Internet-caused schoolwork problems were found to have spent five times more hours online than those who do not. They were also significantly more likely to report that their Internet use caused them to stay up late at night, get less sleep, and miss class.

Kubey, Robert, Michael Lavin, and John Barrows. "Internet Use and Collegiate Academic Performance Decrements: Early Findings." *Journal of Communication.* June 2001.

Another study shows that students are online looking to connect with others:
· College Internet users are twice as likely to use instant messaging on any given day compared to the average Internet user.
· College students are frequently looking for e-mail, with 72% checking e-mail at least once a day.
· 42% of college students say they use the Internet primarily to communicate socially.

Jones, Steve, et al. "The Internet Goes to College: How Students are Living in the Future with Today's Technology." Pew Internet & American Life Project. September 15, 2002.

ONCE UPON A CAMPUS

I would find myself endlessly fascinated by the texture of my floor if it meant not studying.

GRADUATE, ART AND DESIGN, LAGRANGE COLLEGE

You can procrastinate by just staring at your pencil and daydreaming over your Chemistry text-book.

GRADUATE, MATH, CARLETON COLLEGE

I HAVE BEEN CALLED THE "QUEEN OF PROCRASTINATION." I actually can't write papers ahead of time, unless the class requires me to turn in an outline and a rough draft. I tend to start essays at about 10 P.M. or 11 P.M. the night before they are due and pull an all-nighter. It sounds horrible, but I produce my best work when I'm under that kind of pressure.

GRADUATE, SOCIOLOGY, UNIVERSITY OF HAWAII—MANOA

IT WAS FUN WHILE IT LASTED . . .

"I don't need to study tonight—I'll do it in the morning when I get up at 5 A.M." YEAH, RIGHT!

GRADUATE, MASS COMMUNICATIONS, NORTHEASTERN STATE UNIVERSITY

I struggled with procrastination for my first two years of college. Once I quit procrastinating and learned to keep up with my studying, I found that my life is much more enjoyable and my classes are a lot less stressful.

JUNIOR, BIOCHEMISTRY, UNIVERSITY OF CALIFORNIA—LOS ANGELES

My best papers were ones I wrote earlier than the day before they were due. If you do need to put off a paper until the night before it's due, at least do the readings or other prep work for it ahead of time.

SENIOR, ANTHROPOLOGY, UNIVERSITY OF TORONTO

I wish I wouldn't have procrastinated so much. It made some things harder than they had to be.

In two longitudinal studies, psychologists Dianne M. Tice and Roy F. Baumeister found that "students who procrastinate reported lower stress levels and fewer illnesses as semesters began. But when papers came due and exams were scheduled toward the end of the semester, procrastinators reported higher stress levels and more illnesses—indeed, they were physically sicker overall than students who didn't procrastinate."

Berg, Michael. "Psych Yourself for Studying." *www.student.com*. University of Massachusetts—Amherst. 2001.

15

NOSE TO THE GRINDSTONE

Unhook the phone line, turn off the cell phone, get lost in the library, wear comfortable clothes.

SENIOR, POLITICAL SCIENCE/CHINESE LANGUAGE,
UNIVERSITY OF CALIFORNIA—IRVINE

GET OUT OF YOUR ROOM . . .

I had a job where all I did was answer phones, and if I didn't have anything to do while I was there, I would go crazy! So, I brought my homework with me to work, and all I did was study in between phone calls. I got really good grades as a result.

SENIOR, PSYCHOLOGY, UNIVERSITY OF MARYLAND—COLLEGE PARK

The only class in which I aced both tests was the one where my study group met in a bar the night before each test. Whoever couldn't answer the questions had to buy a round.

GRADUATE, CORPORATE COMMUNICATIONS, UNIVERSITY OF HOUSTON

I'd go to a 24-hour diner far away from campus where I knew nobody else would be and stay till the sun came up. (You think I'm exaggerating, don't you?)

GRADUATE, POLITICAL SCIENCE, UNIVERSITY OF CALIFORNIA—SAN DIEGO

TRENT'S SURVIVAL TIP

College kids tend to get up late in the morning. That's a waste of time. If you can get started at 7 A.M. or 8 A.M. every day, it's like you've got an eight-day week.

I lock myself in the silent floors of the library. **ONCE YOU GET A COUPLE OF BAD GRADES IT'S NOT HARD TO FORCE YOURSELF TO SIT DOWN AND WORK.**

SENIOR, GOVERNMENT, UNIVERSITY OF VIRGINIA

I sat among the stacks in the research library so there was nothing else to look at.

GRADUATE, JEWISH STUDIES, UNIVERSITY OF CALIFORNIA—LOS ANGELES

I went to the library or study lounge . . . when people around you are studying, it's easier to get motivated.

GRADUATE, ENGLISH/AMERICAN STUDIES, UNIVERSITY OF NOTRE DAME

Form study sessions even if you're the weak link. The top students always show up and everyone usually does well.

GRADUATE, ENGLISH, MOREHOUSE COLLEGE

Scheduling study groups is a good idea because it forces you to look over the material before you meet so you don't look stupid.

SENIOR, GOVERNMENT, UNIVERSITY OF VIRGINIA

Study groups were very beneficial to me since I tend to procrastinate when I'm by myself. Meeting regularly with a group of classmates keeps you on your toes because you never want to be the freeloader.

GRADUATE, MICROBIOLOGY/SOCIOLOGY, UNIVERSITY OF OKLAHOMA

I always had study marathons before midterms and finals. I would join study groups and we would all study for a few hours, then take a coffee break, then study for a few more hours. If you study with people you like, it is a lot more bearable, and sometimes it's even fun.

JUNIOR, BIOCHEMISTRY, UNIVERSITY OF CALIFORNIA—LOS ANGELES

IT'S A ZEN THING

I SHUT MY COMPUTER OFF AND WENT INTO SOLITARY CONFINEMENT.

GRADUATE, AMERICAN CIVILIZATIONS, BROWN UNIVERSITY

I cleared my mind and distanced myself from people who had other agendas. I surrounded myself with others who valued studying.

GRADUATE, ENGLISH, GEORGIA STATE UNIVERSITY

I never had to force myself to study. I tried to structure things to avoid working right up to a deadline. When this happened I just resigned myself to pulling a late- or all-nighter.

GRADUATE, HISTORY/AMERICAN STUDIES, COLBY COLLEGE

148

I make sure that I have incentives like, "Once I finish this I can take a break . . ." to get ice cream, watch a movie, or anything that sounds appealing.

SENIOR, PRE-LAW, UNIVERSITY OF ILLINOIS—URBANA-CHAMPAIGN

I make a schedule with check boxes and check off each of the boxes as I finish my tasks. It always feels very rewarding to cross off something from my list!

SENIOR, LEGAL STUDIES/SOCIOLOGY, UNIVERSITY OF WISCONSIN

I sit in my La-Z-Boy and I don't let myself stop reading even to go to the bathroom until I get through the present chapter. You'd be amazed how fast you can read with a full bladder.

SENIOR, BIOLOGY, SEATTLE PACIFIC UNIVERSITY

THE GREAT MOTIVATOR

I forced myself to face the prospect of failing and hated it so much that I just knew I had to sit and study.

SENIOR, PSYCHOLOGY, UNIVERSITY OF PENNSYLVANIA

The fear of making a bad grade and thinking about not getting into medical school forced me to study. Fear is a strong force that can really make you get motivated to study.

JUNIOR, BIOLOGY, UNIVERSITY OF ILLINOIS—URBANA-CHAMPAIGN

Just thinking that my parents were shelling out gobs and gobs of money for me to be there was motivation enough. I didn't want to have to deal with Dad—minus $25,000—if I got a D.

GRADUATE, CHEMICAL ENGINEERING, UNIVERSITY OF VIRGINIA

I remind myself that my GPA isn't so hot and I need to improve it to have any chance of getting into med or grad school. I also have a stuffed black cat with big yellow eyes sitting by my computer that stares at me and scares me into studying when I'm trying to goof off at the computer.

SENIOR, BIOCHEMISTRY/ENGLISH, UNIVERSITY OF CALIFORNIA—DAVIS

I KEEP MY GOALS VISUAL, whether that's my screen saver with a quote or a piece of paper with my name on it and the initials "MD" written after it—anything to keep me on track toward reaching my goal.

JUNIOR, BIOLOGICAL SCIENCES, UNIVERSITY OF NEBRASKA—LINCOLN

REALITY BITES

I worked in a factory between my freshman and sophomore years. My dad reminded me that if I didn't finish college that is where I would end up. That helped.

GRADUATE, BIOCHEMISTRY/SPANISH, UNIVERSITY OF WISCONSIN—MADISON

I choose the most pathetic adult in the family and then picture myself being him or her. I know, there's more than one in the family . . . sometimes it's hard to choose.

JUNIOR, ACCOUNTING, CALIFORNIA STATE UNIVERSITY—SACRAMENTO

TO FORCE MYSELF TO STUDY I REMIND MYSELF WHAT FLIPPING BURGERS AT McDONALD'S WOULD BE LIKE.

JUNIOR, BIOCHEMISTRY, VIRGINIA POLYTECHNIC INSTITUTE AND STATE UNIVERSITY

I make a schedule and tell myself that I have to get through a certain amount of work before I go to bed each night. It gets easier as you get older, because everyone's majors get more demanding, so there are less people to fool around with.

SENIOR, BIOLOGY, BUCKNELL UNIVERSITY

A study by Professor Patricia Devine at the University of California at Los Angeles found that "students who visualized their work step-by-step . . . were about 20 percent more likely to start on time and twice as likely to finish on time [than those who didn't visualize their work step-by-step]—in fact, about 80 percent finished before their deadline. . . . The secret: When you visualize each step required to achieve an end result, you are forced to plan and you practically can't help but get your work done in a timely manner."

Berg, Michael. "Psych Yourself for Studying." *www.student.com*. University of Massachusetts–Amherst. 2001.

Wait for that particular inspiration called **LAST MINUTE PANIC.**

GRADUATE, BIOLOGY, UNIVERSITY OF VIRGINIA

16

MAKING THE GRADE: TESTS AND PAPERS

In college, there are only two or three tests and/or papers in a semester-long class, so you have to do really well on all of them to do well in the class. You have to be prepared enough to know from the very start how the professor is going to ask you questions on a test or how the professor wants you to write a paper.

JUNIOR, COGNITIVE SCIENCE, UNIVERSITY OF VIRGINIA

TEST YOUR KNOWLEDGE

"Over prepare" for your first round of tests.

GRADUATE, POLITICAL SCIENCE, TEXAS A&M UNIVERSITY

THE FIRST COLLEGE EXAM YOU TAKE IS MOST LIKELY GOING TO KILL YOU. IT'S NORMAL. YOU USE THAT PAINFUL REALIZATION AND CHANNEL IT INTO MOTIVATION TO PREPARE FOR THE NEXT ONE.

JUNIOR, BIOLOGY/CHEMISTRY, HOUSTON BAPTIST UNIVERSITY

When they say that you can study for one test and fail it, and you can not study for another test and ace it, it's so true. You would be amazed.

GRADUATE, BUSINESS ADMINISTRATION, FLORIDA AGRICULTURAL AND MECHANICAL UNIVERSITY

Start studying from day one and don't let up. Try to synthesize and apply the information, not memorize it.

JUNIOR, BIOLOGY, UNIVERSITY OF MICHIGAN—ANN ARBOR

Take a good composition class at the beginning of school because most of the tests are essay tests.

GRADUATE, LITERATURE, FLORIDA INTERNATIONAL UNIVERSITY

I think one of the most important things that I've learned is to really listen and understand during lectures. Don't just copy exactly what the professor says or writes, paraphrase to insure your understanding. It really cuts down on confusion when you sit down later and try to re-learn your notes.

JUNIOR, BIOLOGY/CHEMISTRY, HOUSTON BAPTIST UNIVERSITY

Ask professors whether the focus of the test will be on the book, the notes, or both, and ask for study guides.

GRADUATE, SPEECH-LANGUAGE PATHOLOGY, TOWSON UNIVERSITY

FIND THE SMART PERSON IN CLASS AND STUDY WITH HIM. *He will be easy to spot: He will ask questions and most likely take lots of notes. If you are the smart one, find someone who is having trouble—you will help someone and strengthen your own knowledge by explaining the concepts to your study partner.*

GRADUATE, BIOPSYCHOLOGY, UNIVERSITY OF MICHIGAN

Talk to upperclassmen about getting old examples of tests and papers.

GRADUATE, CLARINET PERFORMANCE, VASSAR COLLEGE

Don't think you can get away with studying for just one or two nights before you have a big midterm or final exam—it doesn't work. I LEARNED THE HARD WAY. I tried that on my first Biology exam and got a D-. That is the lowest grade I've ever received in college. From then on I knew I needed to change my approach if I was gonna make the grade (no pun intended). That same semester I ended up making the Dean's List.

SENIOR, BIOLOGY, COLLEGE OF WILLIAM & MARY

IT'S SINK OR SWIM; EITHER YOU'LL FIGURE IT OUT OR YOU WON'T. *Studying is more about determination than about technique, because everyone's method is different. If you're determined to find your method, you will.*

SENIOR, BIOLOGY/VOCATIONAL MINISTRY, OKLAHOMA CHRISTIAN UNIVERSITY

SEPPY'S SURVIVAL TIP

If your work starts to get overwhelming, try these campus resources:

· **A writing clinic.** Nobody's prepared for the amount of writing that they're going to be hit with in college.

· **A department clinic.** This is useful if you're looking for specific help in your major.

· **A tutor.** Look for TAs or older students to help you.

Figure out how to write a college paper as soon as possible. This includes actually coming up with something interesting/original to say, picking out quotes from the text, and, **FOR EXTRA PIZZAZZ, ADDING QUOTES FROM OUTSIDE SOURCES AND USING BEAUTIFUL VOCABULARY AND SENTENCE STRUCTURE.**

GRADUATE, ETHNIC STUDIES/HISTORY, BROWN UNIVERSITY

Utilize the writing center on your campus. Those people have experience in writing and can definitely help you improve your writing skills and papers.

GRADUATE, NEAR EASTERN AND JUDAIC STUDIES, BRANDEIS UNIVERSITY

Ask for help from teachers. Ask them for examples of what they're looking for. ("So what would an A paper look like?")

GRADUATE, PSYCHOLOGY, UNIVERSITY OF ALABAMA

DON'T WRITE EXACTLY WHAT THE TEACHER SAID. **ADD YOUR OWN THOUGHTS TO THE MIX.**

GRADUATE, HISTORY/ANTHROPOLOGY, UNIVERSITY OF PENNSYLVANIA

SEPPY'S SURVIVAL TIP

If you're worried about not making the grade in writing, check out *The Nuts and Bolts of College Writing* (nutsandboltsguide.com). This extensive website includes sections on thinking, style, structure, evidence, and mechanics. You can find information on the top ten mistakes made in college writing, how to adhere to MLA style, and the details of plagiarism and how to avoid it.

LEARN HOW TO WRITE DURING YOUR FIRST SEMESTER IN COLLEGE. Invest time in your freshman writing course! Writing in college is completely different from high school, and the most common comments from freshmen are about how their high school teachers loved their writing, but now in college they are doing horribly on their writing assignments.

GRADUATE, SPEECH-LANGUAGE PATHOLOGY, TOWSON UNIVERSITY

Don't be afraid to ask professors about rough drafts, but **be an active asker.** Don't just hand in a rough draft: ask questions about your style, choice of words, etc.

GRADUATE, GOVERNMENT/GERMAN STUDIES, SMITH COLLEGE

Always have at least two other people (preferably older and with more writing experience than you) help you revise your papers before turning them in.

GRADUATE, BIOCHEMISTRY/SPANISH, UNIVERSITY OF WISCONSIN—MADISON

Set your own deadline for three to five days before the paper is actually due. On that day have a *final* draft completed. Leave it alone for a day or two and then come back to it. **This will give you perspective on your own work** and help you avoid writing the paper all on the last night.

GRADUATE, BIOPSYCHOLOGY, UNIVERSITY OF MICHIGAN

NEVER TURN IN A PAPER THAT HASN'T BEEN PROOFREAD BY TWO OR THREE PEOPLE. *You may think you're error-free, but you'll be surprised by what you overlooked the night before while dozing off at the computer.*

GRADUATE, ENGLISH, MOREHOUSE COLLEGE

ONCE UPON A CAMPUS

17

GETTING PUMPED FOR EXAMS

Eat, study, eat, study, sleep, eat, study.

JUNIOR, CHEMICAL BIOLOGY, STEVENS INSTITUTE OF TECHNOLOGY

Start studying after the 11 P.M. episode of *Friends,* get coffee around 2:30 A.M. to stop feeling sleepy, eat spaghetti around 4 A.M., go to sleep for 45 minutes, wake up and shower, and review notes until test time.

GRADUATE, PSYCHOLOGY, NEW YORK UNIVERSITY

Study and then take a long hot shower. The shower gives you a chance to let the information mull around in your head, and the hot water seems to make the info soak into your brain.

SENIOR, BIOLOGY, MILLSAPS COLLEGE

Coffee. Lots of coffee. And continuous breaks so I didn't lose my mind. Sometimes I did these things with friends at the library. After a few hours we'd break and eat lunch together and then resume work.

GRADUATE, EARLY CHILDHOOD AND ELEMENTARY EDUCATION, NEW YORK UNIVERSITY

I ALWAYS WORE GLASSES FOR THE WHOLE WEEK DURING EXAMS. They made me look smarter if, for some reason, all the studying didn't work.

SENIOR, PSYCHOLOGY/CRIMINAL JUSTICE, INDIANA UNIVERSITY—BLOOMINGTON

On the day of the exam, I would wear either my Bio-Sci Club T-shirt or my honors program T-shirt to try to feel smarter.

SENIOR, BIOCHEMISTRY/ENGLISH, UNIVERSITY OF CALIFORNIA—DAVIS

I would get a good rest before taking any exams. Study your material the night before the exam: **SLEEP DEPRIVATION CAN BE A FACTOR ON YOUR PERFORMANCE.** I also performed voodoo rituals . . . just kidding.

JUNIOR, ACCOUNTING, CALIFORNIA STATE UNIVERSITY—SACRAMENTO

It used to be that my friends and I would order Domino's Pizza and Cinnasticks, along with about three million Diet Cokes. Then we would each write a page of our paper and after each page we would watch a movie and eat our food. This might explain why many of my papers took on movie themes or quotes. Now, I just get it over with. **PAPER WRITING IS NO LONGER RITUALISTIC AND FREAKY WHEN YOU'RE A SENIOR, IT'S JUST A PAIN.**

SENIOR, GENDER STUDIES/RELIGIOUS STUDIES, BROWN UNIVERSITY

I LISTEN TO SOME GOOD PUNK ROCK BEFORE I DO ANYTHING ACADEMIC.

GRADUATE, BUSINESS ADMINISTRATION, UNIVERSITY OF FLORIDA

You've probably heard of "The Mozart Effect," a hotly debated topic that claims the use of music can improve memory and enhance spatial reasoning, among other things. Whether or not music makes you smarter, it can be a great break from the grind and a good tension reliever. So pop your favorite CD into your stereo and find out whether or not grooving to your favorite songs while studying works for you.

GET PUMPED UP WITH MUSIC. MY FRIENDS AND I CALL IT THE "GROOVE TECHNIQUE." When you get stressed in the middle of a test, just sit back for a second and groove with the music that became engraved in your head after letting the CD player sit on repeat for forty minutes.

SENIOR, GENETICS, IOWA STATE UNIVERSITY

The night before a big exam I listen to jazz, stretch, and go to bed early.

JUNIOR, BIOLOGY, UNIVERSITY OF MICHIGAN—ANN ARBOR

On the way to the test I turn my car radio up really loud and sing at the top of my lungs to relieve tension.

JUNIOR, BIOCHEMISTRY, VIRGINIA POLYTECHNIC INSTITUTE AND STATE UNIVERSITY

My exams were always at night, so I'd try to eat dinner about three hours earlier than usual to give my food time to digest. **I'D MAKE SURE TO EAT A LIGHT MEAL, TOO—NOTHING TOO HEAVY.**

SENIOR, CHEMISTRY, CORNELL UNIVERSITY

I made sure I didn't eat anything before an exam and always had one of my friends wish me luck.

GRADUATE, BIOLOGY, UNIVERSITY OF CALIFORNIA—LOS ANGELES

Always eat breakfast and always look over key points before the exam.

SENIOR, FINANCE, MIAMI UNIVERSITY

RELAX, YOU'VE GOT IT COVERED

Shut the books the night before the test and get a good night's rest. Relax on the morning of the test. Remember the main points and don't worry about the details. Stay calm; **STRESS WILL ONLY DETRACT FROM WHAT YOU KNOW.**

GRADUATE, SOCIOLOGY, MILLS COLLEGE

Start studying early (a few days in advance), then do a big overall review the night before the test. On the morning of the exam, have a good breakfast with orange juice, pack your bag, and get to class early. Take some gum and water; the act of swallowing seems to make people relax. Go in there knowing that you prepared yourself.

JUNIOR, MICROBIOLOGY AND CELL SCIENCE, UNIVERSITY OF FLORIDA

18

THE PERFECT FIT: COURSE SELECTION, SCHEDULES, AND MAJORS

You have to ask yourself, "What class is going to get me out of bed at eight o'clock in the morning?" That is a class you should definitely sign up for.

SENIOR, BIOMEDICAL SCIENCES, MARQUETTE UNIVERSITY

SPARK YOUR INTELLECT

I firmly believe that you go to college to grow academically, socially, and individually. Therefore I think it is imperative to take classes that further your personal interests as much as your academic interests, even if it means you don't graduate within four years. College is supposed to be the "time of your life" and you should have no regrets, so indulging your curiosities are as important as fulfilling your academic curriculum—take a history of film class if it pleases your heart.

SENIOR, JOURNALISM, UNIVERSITY OF TEXAS—AUSTIN

THIS IS COLLEGE; FIND WHAT YOU LOVE AND DO IT. IF YOU'RE NOT SURE WHAT YOU LOVE, MAINTAIN VARIETY AND YOU'LL FIND IT.

GRADUATE, POLITICAL SCIENCE, COLORADO STATE UNIVERSITY

Pick courses that will still be interesting two and a half months into the semester. If it doesn't sound interesting in August, just think how much you'll hate it in November.

SENIOR, PHILOSOPHY, STATE UNIVERSITY OF NEW YORK—UNIVERSITY AT ALBANY

SCREW PRACTICALITY. Take classes you'll enjoy. No major is going to prepare you for a job.

GRADUATE, FILM, BRIGHAM YOUNG UNIVERSITY

Ask yourself these questions: "Is this going to be beneficial to my future career?" "Is this going to be beneficial to my understanding of the world?" "What interests me most?" "Will I be challenged?"

GRADUATE, BIOLOGY, SAINT JOSEPH'S UNIVERSITY

Pick classes where you are going to use the information—don't pick silly things like French Basket Weaving. What is that going to do for you later?

GRADUATE, HEALTH AND SOCIETY, UNIVERSITY OF ROCHESTER

Have a desire to learn the subject material—if you don't like the topic, it doesn't matter how good the teacher is, you won't get anything out of doing the work.

SENIOR, FILM, NORTHWESTERN UNIVERSITY

When picking courses, especially hard ones, I tried to stop and think: Down the road, will I regret not taking this class just because it is hard and I don't want to work that much? Don't let laziness now make you regretful later.

SENIOR, BIOLOGY, COLLEGE OF WILLIAM & MARY

You are going to have to take an 8 A.M. class, so accept it. An 8 A.M. class with a "good" professor is better than a noon class with a "bad" one.

GRADUATE, BIOLOGY, COLLEGE OF CHARLESTON

TRENT'S SURVIVAL TIP

I think it's fine to drop a course. I think you ought to evaluate, though, why it is that happened. If you start doing it regularly, it's probably a reflection of more than the difficulty of the course.

Never miss an opportunity to ask other students which professors they have taken classes from and what they thought about the professors and the classes. A good professor is the most important factor in choosing classes, and information from former students is the most valuable resource when choosing classes.

SENIOR, POLITICAL SCIENCE, UNIVERSITY OF CALIFORNIA—SAN DIEGO

Ask seniors and juniors—they'll know whose classes to take. And don't just take the "easy" ones, take the teachers that you _learn_ from. You're an adult now—try to think about the long term.

GRADUATE, BIOLOGY, UNIVERSITY OF CENTRAL FLORIDA

You should try to get in contact with any recent alumni or current students of the school that you will be attending to pick their brains and get the background on professors.

GRADUATE, ENGLISH/MUSIC, COLLEGE OF WILLIAM & MARY

Check out a publication like *CAPE* (Course and Professor Evaluations), a book put out by a student-run organization that gives approval ratings of every course and professor, including how many hours of work per week, the difficulty of exams, and other things students had to say about their classes.

GRADUATE, PSYCHOLOGY, UNIVERSITY OF CALIFORNIA—SAN DIEGO

You should read the course descriptions, know of the professor, and know what you're getting into for each class. It saves hassles later on during the semester.

GRADUATE, SOCIOLOGY, UNIVERSITY OF HAWAII—MANOA

Trent Says:

When you're choosing classes always consider these four factors:
· The quality of the professors.
· Whether you're interested in the subject.
· Where it gets you in terms of graduate school.
· Whether it's required for your major or the core curriculum.

Seppy Says:

When selecting classes, make sure you:
· Don't overload on too many hard classes in one semester.
· Do your homework on the professors. The goal is to find professors who match your style and try to take classes with them. After all, you're spending 3,000 bucks on each class in most cases and you've got to think of it as an investment. Think of how many times people try on a $60 sweater before buying it; do the same thing when picking classes.
· Take a variety of classes during your freshman year. Don't take all lectures or all seminars.

SELECTIVE SCHEDULE

Are you really going to be able to make an 8 A.M. class?

GRADUATE, LEGAL STUDIES, UNIVERSITY OF MASSACHUSETTS—AMHERST

ALWAYS GET MORNING CLASSES, IF POSSIBLE. That way, you will
have the rest of the day to study or hang out and it feels like more time is available than when you're cramming for afternoon classes.

GRADUATE, ENGLISH, MOREHOUSE COLLEGE

Unlike most students, **I LIKED TO SPREAD MY CLASSES OUT THROUGH THE DAY.** I found this gave me time to study or complete work in between classes and, let's face it, I also had nothing better to do.

GRADUATE, BUSINESS ADMINISTRATION, UNIVERSITY OF FLORIDA

SEPPY'S SURVIVAL TIP

Think about how much time you have between classes and other commitments rather than trying to always end up with four-day weekends. You can use this time to study, instead of wasting four days trying to force yourself to study. This way you have a ready-made study schedule.

TRENT'S SURVIVAL TIP

If you schedule your classes back-to-back to get them over with, you might waste the rest of the day. If you schedule a class and then have three hours before another class, you'd have three hours to study. Since you have to be around anyway, what's the point of going back to the dorm to do something else?

Avoid big gaps in your schedule. It's nice to be able to go on to campus once and come back after your classes are all done.

GRADUATE, MOLECULAR CELL BIOLOGY, UNIVERSITY OF CALIFORNIA — BERKELEY

BALANCING ACT

Try to spread out the classes you'll really like with the ones you know you'll hate, so you won't have extreme burnout semesters with nothing but difficult, boring classes.

GRADUATE, PSYCHOLOGY, EAST TENNESSEE STATE UNIVERSITY

SPEND YOUR FIRST QUARTER ADJUSTING; TAKE A MODERATE AMOUNT OF UNITS YOUR FIRST YEAR; TAKE YOUR SECOND AND THIRD YEARS VERY SERIOUSLY (LOAD UP ON UNITS); THEN RELAX YOUR LAST YEAR.

SENIOR, POLITICAL SCIENCE/CHINESE LANGUAGE, UNIVERSITY OF CALIFORNIA—IRVINE

I made the mistake of taking all of my general requirements in the first two years and when I became an upperclassman, **I WAS STUCK WITH ALL MY HIGH-LEVEL CLASSES AT ONCE.** *It is difficult to raise your GPA when you have all Biology classes in one quarter. I should have consulted my adviser more, but I thought I knew what I was doing on my own.*

JUNIOR, BIOLOGY, OHIO STATE UNIVERSITY

Balance hard classes with easier ones, or creative classes with technical ones, or science classes with literature ones. **IT'S SO IMPORTANT TO TAKE A VARIETY OF CLASSES** because when the exams kick in, it's more refreshing to switch from a paper in one subject to a paper in another.

GRADUATE, INTERNATIONAL RELATIONS, BROWN UNIVERSITY

Don't take the most time-consuming classes all in one semester. I, for example, learned the hard way when I signed up for three writing component classes at once and ended up having to withdraw from one mid-semester.

GRADUATE, PSYCHOLOGY, UNIVERSITY OF TEXAS—AUSTIN

FULFILLING REQUIREMENTS

Find out *exactly* what your major requires, **MEET WITH AN ADVISER,** and work out your entire schedule for the next four years. That way you don't end up with tons of useless classes and have to spend a fifth year catching up.

SENIOR, POLITICAL SCIENCE, UNIVERSITY OF CALIFORNIA—DAVIS

Planning out my major helped a lot when the enrollment period came around. Try to anticipate little surprises. For example, smaller schools like mine don't offer every course every year, so plan ahead. No one wants to get to senior year and find out that a required class won't be offered that year.

SENIOR, BIOLOGY/VOCATIONAL MINISTRY, OKLAHOMA CHRISTIAN UNIVERSITY

Once you figure out your major, take the requisite courses. I could have graduated early, but I was not able to enroll in all of the classes I needed because in my freshman year I took more of a broad curriculum instead of being more focused on my major.

GRADUATE, INTERNATIONAL STUDIES/RUSSIAN, JOHNS HOPKINS UNIVERSITY

So many people love to pick fun electives or take a lighter course load to insure straight As. If you have half a decade to spare for college, go ahead, have fun and take it easy. If you're like most people, **remember that you need to graduate someday soon!** Talk with counselors so you don't overlook crucial courses that won't show up "missing" till you apply for graduation—that happens to *a lot* of people.

GRADUATE, PSYCHOLOGY/UNIVERSITY SCHOLARS PROGRAM, XAVIER UNIVERSITY

It is very important to make sure that if you're taking a class to fulfill a requirement, it actually fills the requirement. My friends and I have completed horrible classes only to realize that we didn't even need to take them. You can clear up this confusion by speaking to your adviser.

SENIOR, COMMUNICATION, ARIZONA STATE UNIVERSITY

MAJOR DRAMA

I came into college as a business major because I thought it was a good route to take. WRONG! I ended up taking classes I wasn't interested in and, therefore, I did *horribly,* which killed my GPA. So if you're not sure what you want to do, there's *nothing* wrong with saying that your major is "undecided."

SENIOR, FAMILY STUDIES, MIAMI UNIVERSITY (OHIO)

MY BIGGEST REGRET WAS NOT HAVING A SET DIRECTION IN COLLEGE. *For the first two years, I had no clue what I wanted to do. By the time I made up my mind, I had to take all my courses for my major so my last two years were filled with all the difficult courses.*

GRADUATE, ECONOMICS, NEW YORK UNIVERSITY

I will soon be entering medical school and I thought that since I was pre-med I had to major in science. However, that is not the case. **I WILL BE TAKING SCIENCE FOR THE REST OF MY LIFE, SO I SHOULD HAVE DONE SOMETHING DIFFERENT AT THE TIME.** I would have been fine with just a science minor.

GRADUATE, BIOLOGY/FLUTE, HOUGHTON COLLEGE

CHOOSING A MAJOR

Seppy Says:

It doesn't matter what you major in. Pick something that really interests you.

If you really want to go to medical school, that doesn't mean you have to be a Biology major—in fact you're probably better off *not* majoring in Bio. Take all the right pre-med classes, but major in something else.

There are so many schools now where you can create your own major. I think that's way cool. It's a great opportunity to synthesize your varied interests.

Trent Says:

Don't try to pick your major too soon; rather, take a bunch of different courses in a bunch of different fields first.

I would discourage you from pursuing a double major just because it looks good on paper. If you apply to grad school or try for a job with a great GPA in History, you're far better off than if you have an okay GPA with a double major in History and English. Careerwise, in most cases, your major doesn't matter.

19

LEARNING FROM THE EXPERTS

Remember that professors and teacher's assistants are people, too. They are often a great source of wisdom and expertise.

GRADUATE, BIOLOGY, MIDLAND LUTHERAN COLLEGE

JUST YOUR AVERAGE JOE

College professors are normal people. Some are kind, some are jerks, some are smart, some are brilliant, some are awful teachers, some are superb instructors. You have to accept that and approach them accordingly. TAs are mutants; cross your fingers and hope they're normal.

JUNIOR, PHILOSOPHY, NORTHWESTERN UNIVERSITY

Professors and teacher's assistants genuinely care that you're learning. They're not there to ruin your life (a misconception we all had in high school). **THEY'RE THERE BECAUSE THEY ARE PASSIONATE ABOUT WHAT THEY'RE TEACHING YOU, AND THEY WANT YOU TO SEE WHY THEY LOVE WHAT THEY'RE TEACHING.** *Show them that you care about what you're learning—not just to get a good grade but because you're interested in the subject.*

GRADUATE, BIOMETRY AND STATISTICS, CORNELL UNIVERSITY

Most professors truly want to help you, however, there are those who seem like they want nothing more than to watch you fail. **Don't let those professors get you down. Work harder to succeed despite them. Trust me, it feels good when you do.**

SENIOR, BIOLOGY, MARY WASHINGTON COLLEGE

Just because they're great lecturers doesn't mean they have great people skills. And just because they're bad lecturers doesn't mean they have bad people skills.

GRADUATE, POLITICAL SCIENCE, UNIVERSITY OF CALIFORNIA—SAN DIEGO

LEARN WHAT THEY WANT AND GIVE IT TO THEM.

SENIOR, BIOLOGY, TOWSON UNIVERSITY

Professors like to have feedback when teaching a class. They also like to know that the students are prepared for the class.

SENIOR, BIOCHEMISTRY, CITY UNIVERSITY OF NEW YORK—LEHMAN COLLEGE

Professors want respect. If your professor has a PhD, you should remember that when you address him.

GRADUATE, BUSINESS ADMINISTRATION, UNIVERSITY OF FLORIDA

Show you're trying, even if it's an e-mail before a test asking a question you already know the answer to. They love feeling like they are important and actually teaching you things outside of the classroom.

GRADUATE, SOCIOLOGY/FAMILY STUDIES AND HUMAN DEVELOPMENT, UNIVERSITY OF ARIZONA

Do not approach a professor by asking what will be on the test. It is saying that you are only interested in the grade and not the process of learning.

GRADUATE, BIOCHEMISTRY, UNIVERSITY OF CALIFORNIA—DAVIS

Be early to class—walking in late is very rude. I was amazed at how many times I saw students walk in late *right in front* of a professor who was lecturing. It is also rude to leave class before the lecture is over.

GRADUATE, ECONOMICS/GOVERNMENT AND POLITICS,
UNIVERSITY OF MARYLAND—COLLEGE PARK

Don't ask stupid questions . . . and there are stupid questions.

SENIOR, HISTORY, UNIVERSITY OF NOTRE DAME

TRENT'S SURVIVAL TIP

Don't go to office hours just because you think you ought to go to office hours. You're going to have to prepare and make sure you're asking good questions, or you're just going to annoy the professor or TA who's working with you.

While professors may be busy doing research and working for tenure, **THE TAs ARE AN UNTAPPED SOURCE OF INFORMATION** *and are almost always willing to give you advice, whether it be on courses, professors, or just campus life in general.*

GRADUATE, PSYCHOLOGY AND SOCIAL BEHAVIOR, UNIVERSITY OF CALIFORNIA—IRVINE

TAs are usually cool and will help you out a lot. Professors' office hours are helpful, but don't go if you are clueless about a subject—stick with the TA. You don't want to look bad in front of the person who is going to give you the grade.

JUNIOR, BIOCHEMISTRY, UNIVERSITY OF CALIFORNIA—LOS ANGELES

TAs are just like you and, for the most part, they truly have a passion for what they're teaching. Relate to them on an even level.

GRADUATE, LEGAL STUDIES, UNIVERSITY OF MASSACHUSETTS—AMHERST

ASK AND YOU WILL RECEIVE

Make your professors and TAs talk to you at *your* level and be honest if you don't understand something.

GRADUATE, BIOLOGY, SEATTLE UNIVERSITY

If you ask for help, you'll usually get it—probably more than you asked for.

GRADUATE, POLITICAL SCIENCE, UNIVERSITY OF THE SOUTH

YOU NEED TO KNOW WHO GRADES YOUR WORK, AND GO TO THAT PERSON FOR HELP. *For example, if the professor lectures, but the TA is the one who does all the grading, go to the TA for help with any assignments.*

GRADUATE, SOCIOLOGY, UNIVERSITY OF HAWAII—MANOA

Professors and TAs are pretty accommodating, so make sure that you have good communications with them. They are not mind readers so you have to take the initiative and explain your problem. Most of the time you will be pleased with the result!

GRADUATE, BIOCHEMISTRY, RUTGERS—THE STATE UNIVERSITY OF NEW JERSEY

They sometimes forget what it was like to be in our position, *so talk to them frequently and they will more often take into account your problems and concerns.*

SENIOR, BIOCHEMISTRY/PSYCHOLOGY, BAYLOR UNIVERSITY

YOU HAVE TO COMMUNICATE. Otherwise, they just won't know the difficulties you are facing. Meet with them, e-mail them, leave them notes—whatever it takes.

SENIOR, PSYCHOLOGY, UNIVERSITY OF PENNSYLVANIA

A PROFESSOR WILL NOT FLUNK YOU IF SHE KNOWS YOUR NAME.

GRADUATE, SPORTS MANAGEMENT, UNIVERSITY OF KANSAS

IT'S SIMPLE. SPEAK UP, AND STAND UP FOR YOURSELF. NEVER BE AFRAID.

GRADUATE, BIOLOGY AND NUTRITION, PENNSYLVANIA STATE UNIVERSITY

Be opinionated! Don't just say yes to everything professors and TAs say; they could be wrong sometimes, and if you correct their mistakes they will actually remember you!

JUNIOR, BIOLOGY, STATE UNIVERSITY OF NEW YORK—BINGHAMTON UNIVERSITY

You really just need to get professors and teacher's assistants to notice you and let them know that, regardless of your status in class, you are willing to go the extra mile to do better and that you are open to their ideas.

GRADUATE, POLITICAL SCIENCE, UNIVERSITY OF HAWAII—MANOA

E-mail is the greatest invention ever. They respond very quickly, and it's just so much easier to get your questions answered right away.

JUNIOR, BIOLOGY, COLLEGE OF WILLIAM & MARY

ONCE UPON A CAMPUS

If you show enthusiasm in your instructors' fields or in what they are teaching you, then it will be easy to get their attention. **SIT UP IN FRONT AND RIGHT IN THE MIDDLE OF THE LECTURE HALL.** *If you are really interested in the subject or lecture, use physical communication to show it. Smile and nod your head to show you understand what is being said. Although a freshman might not think it's important for the lecturer to know that she exists, establishing a relationship with one's instructors is very important, and it will pay off tremendously once the time comes to ask those instructors for letters of recommendation to get into grad school.*

SENIOR, PSYCHOLOGY/SOCIAL BEHAVIOR, UNIVERSITY OF CALIFORNIA—IRVINE

If you aren't going to be in class, make a point to write a quick e-mail to your professor. And when you get back, make a point to talk to the professor about what you have missed and explain that you are concerned about falling behind. They will get to know your name, and they will see that you are truly concerned about the course material.

GRADUATE, ENGLISH, GEORGE MASON UNIVERSITY

THEY'VE HEARD EVERY EXCUSE IN THE BOOK. The best thing to do is just tell your professor you didn't feel like coming to class rather than saying, "My great-aunt died and I had to go out of town." Yes, I used this once and I'm not proud of it.

SENIOR, FAMILY STUDIES, MIAMI UNIVERSITY (OHIO)

Be honest. If you missed a class because you slept through it, tell them! They won't be entirely happy, but they'll know that you aren't a liar.

GRADUATE, ENVIRONMENTAL STUDIES, EMORY & HENRY COLLEGE

GAIN THE EXTRA ADVANTAGE

The more your professor knows you, the better. My relationship came in handy when I had an emergency and could not turn something in right on time or could not make it to class.

GRADUATE, POLITICAL SCIENCE/ENGLISH, SPELMAN COLLEGE

I AM THANKFUL THAT I FORMED RELATIONSHIPS WITH MY PROFESSORS. When all is said and done and you've received your degree, they still have an impact on your future. Applying to law or grad schools with a letter of recommendation from Professor Joe Shmoe who "thinks he remembers you" is useless.

GRADUATE, SOCIAL RELATIONS, JAMES MADISON COLLEGE AT MICHIGAN STATE UNIVERSITY

20 LOOKING AHEAD

Employers want to know what your experience is, not what grades you got. Graduate school is a balance between the two. They want to know that you challenged yourself with the classes you picked and that you participated in something besides school.

GRADUATE, CRIMINOLOGY/LAW AND SOCIETY,

UNIVERSITY OF CALIFORNIA—IRVINE

CRAFTING THE PERFECT RÉSUMÉ

I wish I had done a better internship during my senior year or summer breaks. They help you figure out what's out there and what you need to know.

GRADUATE, ENVIRONMENTAL STUDIES, EMORY & HENRY COLLEGE

Get good internships!!! **This is the only time you will be given responsibility without having any experience. Employers and graduate schools will look favorably on these internships.**

GRADUATE, POLITICAL SCIENCE, UNIVERSITY OF CALIFORNIA—SAN DIEGO

Employers who responded to the National Association of Colleges and Employers (NACE) *Job Outlook 2003* survey said that more than 54 percent of their new college hires had internship experience. Government and nonprofit employers said they hire 42.2 percent of their interns for full-time positions.

November 1, 2002

I was overprepared for the job market. I had internships during my summer and January breaks. I also completed a senior thesis and attended conferences so that I had completed a major piece of writing and had presentation experience.

GRADUATE, ENVIRONMENTAL POLICY, SCIENCE, AND VALUES, WELLS COLLEGE

I wish I hadn't concentrated so much on padding my résumé with extracurricular activities; it ended up costing me a better GPA.

GRADUATE, BIOLOGY, COLLEGE OF CHARLESTON

I wish that I had taken a minor in Spanish. **BEING ABLE TO SPEAK TWO LANGUAGES MAKES YOU A BETTER COMMODITY IN THE JOB MARKET.**

GRADUATE, CRIMINAL JUSTICE, WEST CHESTER UNIVERSITY

TIPS ON BUILDING YOUR RÉSUMÉ

Trent Says:

Developing strong writing skills is the most important thing you can do to prepare yourself for the job market. Also, it doesn't matter what industry you go into, grades help.

How important are internships? It depends on what you want to do. If you want to go to medical school or work in politics, they could be important. If you want to work in consumer banking, internships probably are not so important.

Finally, try to do something during the summer that augments your education. Work. Travel. Get an internship. Employers like to see people with varied interests—not just academic pursuits.

Seppy Says:

Distinguish yourself from the rest of the pack. Work on projects where you get some sort of credit. Get your name on a research report or volunteer in your area of interest. Employers and grad schools want people who show some level of focus.

Internships can also be helpful. Try your alumni office or your friends' parents (because they can't hire their own kid, but they can hire you) for leads.

I wish I had networked more with alumni and attended graduate school workshops organized by the university.

GRADUATE, POLITICAL ECONOMY OF INDUSTRIAL SOCIETIES, UNIVERSITY OF CALIFORNIA—BERKELEY

I should have taken advantage of the **MOCK INTERVIEW SESSIONS** offered by the career center.

GRADUATE, ART AND DESIGN, LAGRANGE COLLEGE

I wish I had taken advantage of the career center. I would have been exposed to more companies and had more opportunities to practice interviewing.

GRADUATE, MICROBIOLOGY, INDIANA UNIVERSITY

I wish I had taken a class on writing résumés and cover letters, job strategies, and interviewing skills. **I graduated thinking I would have no problem getting a job, but it's a lot harder than I thought–** I wish someone had prepared me better for that reality.

GRADUATE, CRIMINAL JUSTICE, VITERBO UNIVERSITY

I should have studied the job market more carefully and found out exactly what it is that I want to do. I should have taken advantage of alumni networking and professors to talk about what certain jobs are like.

GRADUATE, INTERNATIONAL STUDIES, BRIGHAM YOUNG UNIVERSITY

Do not wait until the last semester to "line something up." I ALWAYS THOUGHT THAT WHEN YOU BECAME A SENIOR, JOB MARKETERS WOULD FLOCK TO YOUR DOOR *and beg you to sign on for a salary position at some company relating exactly to your major . . . not even close.*

GRADUATE, BIOLOGY, UNIVERSITY OF CENTRAL FLORIDA

I wish I had known which classes would be best to take for my major and the career I wanted to go into.

GRADUATE, BIOLOGY, CLEMSON UNIVERSITY

I wish I had taken the GRE *waaaaay* earlier. I should have taken a prep class back in the early part of my junior year. I'm currently jobless and frantically applying to grad schools.

GRADUATE, PSYCHOLOGY/ORGANIZATIONAL STUDIES, UNIVERSITY OF MICHIGAN—ANN ARBOR

Studying more would have helped me. **I HAD A 3.6 GPA, AND THERE IS NO REASON WHY IT SHOULDN'T HAVE BEEN A 3.9.**

GRADUATE, BIOCHEMISTRY/SPANISH, UNIVERSITY OF WISCONSIN—MADISON

I took college seriously, and I got into law school and I landed a great job. The people who thought college was something they did not have to work for are still looking for a job and did not make it to graduate school.

GRADUATE, CRIMINOLOGY/LAW AND SOCIETY, UNIVERSITY OF CALIFORNIA—IRVINE

Get your recommendations right after you finish a course with a professor as opposed to senior year when you need them. That way, you're fresh in their minds.

GRADUATE, PSYCHOLOGY, CONNECTICUT COLLEGE

I started sending out cover letters and résumés in September of my freshman year and that is the reason I am employed now.

GRADUATE, AMERICAN STUDIES, YALE UNIVERSITY

21 LEARN FROM THEIR REGRETS

I regret that I only truly enjoyed my last year of college. I appreciated where I was and who I was with only when I knew it wasn't going to last.

GRADUATE, COGNITIVE SCIENCE, UNIVERSITY OF VIRGINIA

My biggest regret is that I didn't take advantage of more free concerts, speeches, and events.

GRADUATE, BIOLOGY, INDIANA UNIVERSITY

I regret not taking advantage of everything college has to offer. There were so many speakers and colloquiums, but I was always too busy or too tired. I wish I'd experienced more of the diversity and intellectual environment provided here.

SENIOR, NEUROSCIENCE, UNIVERSITY OF ROCHESTER

MY BIGGEST REGRET IS BLOWING STUFF OFF IN ORDER TO GET WORK DONE. Yes, schoolwork is very important, but there are a lot of other experiences at college that will stay with you forever.

SENIOR, GOVERNMENT, UNIVERSITY OF VIRGINIA

216

I DIDN'T HAVE ENOUGH FUN WHILE I WAS IN COLLEGE. I FOUND THE PERFECT BALANCE OF WORK AND PLAY TOO LATE. FIND IT EARLY!!

GRADUATE, PSYCHOLOGY, UNIVERSITY OF GEORGIA

My biggest regret was getting tied down with a boyfriend for two years—my friends and fun slipped away.

SENIOR, CHEMISTRY, JOHN CARROLL UNIVERSITY

My biggest regret was not joining my sorority sooner! Those girls were my closest friends, and they made my schoolwork so much easier to do. College life as a whole was better just because they were there.

GRADUATE, ENVIRONMENTAL STUDIES, EMORY & HENRY COLLEGE

A CHANGE OF SCENERY?

I transferred from one college to another. **IF I HAD TO DO IT ALL OVER AGAIN, I WOULD HAVE JUST STAYED AT THE FIRST SCHOOL AND WORKED THINGS OUT DIFFERENTLY.** The difference in the new school's curriculum was a big setback. Although all of my credits were transferred, it still took me longer to finish because I had to fulfill the school's requirements.

SENIOR, BIOCHEMISTRY, CITY UNIVERSITY OF NEW YORK—LEHMAN COLLEGE

My biggest regret is not transferring out when I had the chance. Although I have met a few wonderful people, I spent four years of my life in a place that I didn't like very much, where I did not fit in, and where there were very few people I could relate to. If you feel by the middle of your freshman year that you made the wrong decision about which college to attend . . . leave! There's no sense in spending four years of your life being unhappy. It is a pain to fill out transfer applications, but do it on the chance that the next place will be better.

SENIOR, BIOLOGY, MILLSAPS COLLEGE

218

TRANSFERRING TIPS

Seppy Says:

You'd better be sure you want to transfer because it's hard to do. First, you have no connections. When you get to your new school, everyone else is way ahead of you both academically and in forming friendships and you may always feel sort of like a stepchild, on the outside of things. Second, if you're doing well enough academically to get into a new college, you'll probably continue to do well at your current college. So unless there are other factors involved (i.e., social or emotional reasons), I say proceed with caution.

Trent Says:

Never go to a school with the assumption that you'll transfer. If you're going to go to a school, make sure you'll be happy graduating from there. Having said that, if you do want to transfer, know that transfers are not easy— I've known a lot of people who have gone from one school to another who had a hard time figuring out what would transfer between schools. If you're considering transferring, you really do need to know what's involved.

My biggest regret was not going to class a lot my freshman year. I thought that I didn't *need* to go to class since I didn't *have* to, so I usually didn't and I suffered the consequences!

SENIOR, PSYCHOLOGY/PRE-LAW, UNIVERSITY OF ILLINOIS—URBANA-CHAMPAIGN

As crappy as dorms may be, I regret never having the chance to live in one, even if for one semester. You meet so many people in your building.

SENIOR, MICROBIOLOGY AND CELL SCIENCE/CHEMISTRY, UNIVERSITY OF FLORIDA

I regret not changing my major. I thought I had to know what I wanted to do when I got to college, so I stuck with it even though I wasn't satisfied because I was afraid of uncertainty.

SENIOR, FILM, NORTHWESTERN UNIVERSITY

I regret thinking that sororities were an important group to be a part of.

SENIOR, BIOCHEMISTRY AND PSYCHOLOGY, BAYLOR UNIVERSITY

220

My biggest regret from college was graduating. College is an amazing experience. Just try to enjoy each day because the four years will fly by.

GRADUATE, POLITICAL SCIENCE, SAINT JOSEPH'S UNIVERSITY

22 LIFE LESSONS

*Every experience in college gets chalked up to who you are and who you want to be. Becoming **you** is not what you do or what you come in contact with, it is how you handle situations and clearly think your way through them.*

GRADUATE, BIOLOGY, UNIVERSITY OF CENTRAL FLORIDA

I learned that even when I am unsure of myself, if I really try my hardest at something, I can do well.

GRADUATE, SOCIOLOGY, UNIVERSITY OF HAWAII—MANOA

Don't take yourself too seriously. If something seems like a huge failure, very urgent, or stressful, take a step back and look at how important that small event is compared to the whole picture. What seems incredibly important at the time usually isn't worth stressing yourself out about.

GRADUATE, BIOMEDICAL SCIENCES, MARQUETTE UNIVERSITY

Decisions you make for yourself, by yourself, make you the happiest.

GRADUATE, GOVERNMENT/GERMAN STUDIES, SMITH COLLEGE

I have my limits, and I cannot be involved in everything. **I know now not to overwork myself and to make time to work out, relax, and sleep.**

GRADUATE, GOVERNMENT, DARTMOUTH COLLEGE

I learned that I needed to be organized and stay on top of tasks, which is important for all jobs. **I also learned how to interact and work with all types of people,** which—interestingly enough—I didn't learn in the classroom, but through interactions with my peers.

GRADUATE, HEALTH AND SOCIETY, UNIVERSITY OF ROCHESTER

I am capable of any reasonable task that is placed in front of me. I never realized that I could write a one-hundred page senior thesis, but I did so without much difficulty.

GRADUATE, POLITICAL SCIENCE, UNIVERSITY OF FLORIDA

LEARN YOUR LESSON

It's not so much *what* you learn in college that helps you in life, **it's learning *how* to think that will help you out in the long run.** College doesn't teach you the solution to everything, but it teaches you how to come up with a solution on your own.

GRADUATE, BIOMETRY AND STATISTICS, CORNELL UNIVERSITY

I became very humble in college. I realized that there was actually very little about the world that I knew and accepted that as a starting point to a post-college life of learning.

GRADUATE, ENGLISH, CORNELL UNIVERSITY

Knowledge is given by a professor; wisdom comes from your experiences.

GRADUATE, MICROBIOLOGY, INDIANA UNIVERSITY

Knowledge comes in many forms, not just books and lectures.

GRADUATE, SOCIOLOGY/POLITICAL SCIENCE, STATE UNIVERSITY OF NEW YORK—UNIVERSITY AT BUFFALO

If you want to follow your passions, you will have to sacrifice a lot, but in the end you will be happier than the people who are just out for the money.

GRADUATE, BIOLOGY, GEORGETOWN UNIVERSITY

Don't cheat or take the easy road. You will have to struggle for most of the good things in life. Work hard and be proud of your work product.

GRADUATE, POLITICAL SCIENCE, UNIVERSITY OF CALIFORNIA—SAN DIEGO

You're on your own. Someone is not always there to guide you or help you or look out for your best interests. **You have to work hard for what you want.**

GRADUATE, ECONOMICS, NEW YORK UNIVERSITY

I learned that having a role model or mentor helps you get through the day.

GRADUATE, BIOLOGICAL SCIENCES, UNIVERSITY OF CALIFORNIA—DAVIS

WHO YOU KNOW IS MORE IMPORTANT THAN WHAT YOU KNOW.

GRADUATE, BIOLOGY, INDIANA UNIVERSITY

You learn when to say no and when to drop what you're doing to help out. These are good things to know in life.

GRADUATE, PSYCHOLOGY, CONNECTICUT COLLEGE

Pay attention to what you *enjoy* doing; it's a sign about what you *should* be doing.

GRADUATE, PSYCHOLOGY, UNIVERSITY OF CALIFORNIA—SAN DIEGO

LIFE LESSONS

Most people are not quick to do you any favors, but the ones who do are your true friends.

GRADUATE, ENGLISH, UNIVERSITY OF FLORIDA

I CAN'T BE AS IDEALISTIC AS I WAS WHEN I WAS A FROSH—THE REAL WORLD IS PRETTY MEAN.

GRADUATE, POLITICAL SCIENCE, UNIVERSITY OF THE SOUTH

YOU WILL SURVIVE. COLLEGE TEACHES SURVIVAL SKILLS!

GRADUATE, BUSINESS ADMINISTRATION, FLORIDA AGRICULTURAL AND MECHANICAL UNIVERSITY

I KNEW I'D BE ABLE TO SURVIVE COLLEGE WHEN . . .

I got a good grade on my second exam after flunking my first one.

SENIOR, BIOLOGY, COLLEGE OF WILLIAM & MARY

I felt homesick and my new college friends bought me hot chocolate to cheer me up.

SENIOR, COMMUNICATION, UNIVERSITY OF CALIFORNIA—SANTA BARBARA

I saw my neighbor cry about not being able to use the laundry machine.

GRADUATE, BIOLOGY, UNIVERSITY OF CALIFORNIA—LOS ANGELES

I went a week without calling home.

GRADUATE, POLITICAL SCIENCE, TEXAS A&M UNIVERSITY

I'm about to graduate and I'm still not sure I will survive. One day at a time.

SENIOR, SOCIAL WORK, NIAGARA UNIVERSITY

23

REMEMBER THE TIME . . .

One night I was studying with a friend of mine. We were in a study room at our library. Our library has eight floors and we were on the seventh floor. You can see all of Miami from up there. While we were studying, we looked out the window and saw fireworks.

GRADUATE, PSYCHOLOGY, FLORIDA INTERNATIONAL UNIVERSITY

A group of us burned our notes from our Genetics class after a miserable semester. It was good riddance and a great stress reliever. It was a nice way to "let go" and release our angry energy.

SENIOR, BIOLOGY/ENVIRONMENTAL STUDIES, WASHINGTON COLLEGE

Last year I lived in an on-campus apartment with two other girls. We, along with the people in the apartment next to us, threw a Mardi Gras party. We handed out flyers all over campus. The place was so packed that you couldn't move, and the cops broke it up within the first hour. It was quite a success for those few minutes, though!

JUNIOR, BIOLOGY, COLLEGE OF WILLIAM & MARY

Road trips are great. I'll never forget all the road trips I've taken with different girlfriends in college—Omaha, Twin Cities, little hick towns with divey bars. It's all been a blast.

SENIOR, BIOCHEMISTRY AND MOLECULAR BIOLOGY, CORNELL COLLEGE

We don't get much snow in Cincinnati, but during the winter of my sophomore year we had a big storm! I was the resident assistant for our basketball team and many of them were out-of-towners who had never seen snow. **We all bundled up, went outside, and started an enormous snowball fight with the residents of the dorm next door. It was great!** Everyone had homework to do, tests to study for, but they took the time out to throw some snow—it was wonderful.

GRADUATE, PSYCHOLOGY/UNIVERSITY SCHOLARS PROGRAM, XAVIER UNIVERSITY

My most memorable experience would have to be when I spoke before the Board of Regents of the university to urge them to create a Lesbian, Gay, Bisexual, Transgendered Resource Center. I wasn't even out to myself when I went to college.

GRADUATE, COMMUNICATION, EASTERN MICHIGAN UNIVERSITY

My most memorable experience was rallying on campus against violence toward women. It was so cool walking through the campus chanting for women's rights.

GRADUATE, ENGLISH, GEORGE MASON UNIVERSITY

The most memorable experience for me was cheering for the Northwestern-Wisconsin football game in 2000. I have never seen a stadium full of people leave in complete silence. **Victory is sweet, especially when it is achieved with four seconds to go in the game.**

SENIOR, ANTHROPOLOGY/INTERNATIONAL STUDIES, NORTHWESTERN UNIVERSITY

I was coming back one night from an exam that I felt I had done really well on when the first snow of the year started to fall, making it seem so magical.

SENIOR, CHEMISTRY, CORNELL UNIVERSITY

My most memorable experience was getting a 4.0 GPA one semester. I had never done that in high school and **IT WAS ONE OF MY GOALS.**

JUNIOR, ACCOUNTING/FINANCE, WASHINGTON UNIVERSITY IN ST. LOUIS

I passed a test for which I had studied for two weeks straight. It was a big deal because the test was given by a professor who was notorious for his detailed tests. I passed the test hands-down and had expected less. I felt great and **I learned what I was capable of doing.**

GRADUATE, ENGLISH, MOREHOUSE COLLEGE

I traveled to Russia to work in orphanages with some people from my department; it changed my life.

GRADUATE, SPEECH-LANGUAGE PATHOLOGY, TOWSON UNIVERSITY

My school sponsors a program that took me to China, Japan, New Zealand, and Australia during one semester, and it was the time of my life. **If it's at all available, travel for a while during college. It's easier to do in college than later in life.**

SENIOR, BIOLOGY/VOCATIONAL MINISTRY, OKLAHOMA CHRISTIAN UNIVERSITY

My most memorable experience was the summer I spent abroad. I worked for two months in London, completely on my own, and then I studied through a school program at Oxford University. The entire experience was absolutely invaluable; I matured and grew in more ways than I could possibly have foreseen. And a big part of that was just getting far away from everyone and everything that was familiar to me.

GRADUATE, PSYCHOLOGY, UNIVERSITY OF TEXAS—AUSTIN

My most memorable experience was the day I finished up my last term paper and handed it to my professor. As I put it in his hands he very calmly said to me, "You are now a graduate." That is a memory I can never forget.

GRADUATE, SOCIOLOGY/POLITICAL SCIENCE, STATE UNIVERSITY OF NEW YORK—UNIVERSITY AT BUFFALO

At graduation I was honored with an award named after a late professor who meant the world to me.

GRADUATE, ENVIRONMENTAL POLICY, SCIENCE, AND VALUES, WELLS COLLEGE

My most memorable moment was walking out of my last exam senior year. It was bittersweet. **I WANTED TO STAY BECAUSE I LOVED THE LIFE . . . BUT I KNEW IT WAS TIME TO MOVE ON AND I WAS PROUD OF WHAT I HAD DONE.**

GRADUATE, HISTORY, UNIVERSITY OF MASSACHUSETTS

24 THE GOLDEN RULE

Don't pretend to be something you're not. Don't drink just to fit in. Don't wear J.Crew just to fit in. Don't ignore all of your classes just to fit in. Be yourself. There are countless others who will find you fun and exciting just for being you.

SENIOR, BIOLOGY/CHEMISTRY, DENISON UNIVERSITY

INDULGE YOUR HEDONISTIC SIDE . . .

Spontaneity is the key to life. College is the last time you will have the freedom to ditch a Friday class to go snowboarding or skip your 12:40 to meet the boys down at the local pub for wings and beer. Take advantage.

GRADUATE, ANTHROPOLOGY/PRE-MEDICINE, ARIZONA STATE UNIVERSITY

GET YOUR WORK DONE EARLY SO YOU CAN PARTY LATER.

GRADUATE, NEAR EASTERN AND JUDAIC STUDIES, BRANDEIS UNIVERSITY

Be open-minded and take risks and, most importantly, have fun.

SENIOR, BIOMEDICAL SCIENCES, MARQUETTE UNIVERSITY

YOU DON'T HAVE TO COME OUT OF COLLEGE WITH A 4.0 GPA, but it will get you a lot further than a 2.0. So balance your time accordingly.

GRADUATE, BIOLOGY, COLLEGE OF CHARLESTON

Have fun, relax, and enjoy the time while you are there. But don't goof off all the time. **It's expensive to start all over!**

GRADUATE, ENVIRONMENTAL STUDIES, EMORY & HENRY COLLEGE

Watch yourself. It's very easy to get lost in a crowd or dedicate your whole life to having fun. Make sure college work is a priority and don't get behind.

SENIOR, EXERCISE AND MOVEMENT SCIENCE, UNIVERSITY OF OREGON

ONCE UPON A CAMPUS

Don't be misled by the crazy college life you see in movies and on television. They only show the fun and not the consequences. College is about learning and self-discovery. Just remember that going to college is also for the good of your future.

SENIOR, POLITICAL SCIENCE/CHINESE LANGUAGE, UNIVERSITY OF CALIFORNIA—IRVINE

Be accepting. DIVERSITY IS A HUGE PART OF COLLEGE LIFE—prepare yourself for racial, sexual, and religious diversity. It can be a fun learning experience if you keep an open mind.

GRADUATE, POLITICAL SCIENCE/ENGLISH, VIRGINIA POLYTECHNIC INSTITUTE AND STATE UNIVERSITY

Make a thousand-and-one friends. They don't all have to be your best friends, but always know that you have someone to fit that niche that you need filled at that moment. Have workout-buddies, party-buddies, study-buddies, eating-buddies, class-buddies, and more. Everyone has some similar interest and that part of them and that part of you can always hang out.

SENIOR, POLITICAL SCIENCE, UNIVERSITY OF CALIFORNIA—DAVIS

"A record high 70.0 percent of . . . freshmen report having 'socialized with someone of another racial/ethnic group' in the last year. . . . Women remain more likely than men are to socialize with people from racial/ethnic backgrounds that differ from their own."

Sax, Linda J., et al. "The American Freshman: National Norms for Fall 2001." Cooperative Institutional Research Program. 2001.

Get to know yourself first, others later, and everything else in between. Don't let those around you solely mold you; **mold them as well.**

SENIOR, PHYSICS, SPELMAN COLLEGE

Chances are, if you got into college, you have a pretty good head on your shoulders. Use it.

GRADUATE, BIOLOGY, GEORGETOWN UNIVERSITY

Look out for your classmates along the way. They'll repay you in more ways than you could expect!

GRADUATE, POLITICAL SCIENCE, TEXAS A&M UNIVERSITY

Go to class. I don't care how hungover you are, I don't care if you haven't showered, I don't care if you didn't do the work—go. Trust me.

GRADUATE, LEGAL STUDIES, UNIVERSITY OF MASSACHUSETTS—AMHERST

Do your dishes or die a slow and painful death from your housemates' wrath.

SENIOR, NEUROSCIENCE/BEHAVIOR/SCIENCE IN SOCIETY, WESLEYAN UNIVERSITY

ONCE UPON A CAMPUS

Learning in college is two-fold: Learning new subjects and learning how to live.

GRADUATE, PUBLIC RELATIONS, UNIVERSITY OF FLORIDA

Listen. Always be slow to speak, and you'll learn more.

SENIOR, GOVERNMENT/SPANISH, UNIVERSITY OF TEXAS—AUSTIN

Honesty takes you a long way. Cheaters only prosper for so long; they eventually fall.

JUNIOR, ACCOUNTING, CALIFORNIA STATE UNIVERSITY—SACRAMENTO

Keep an open mind. Just because you've never done it, seen it, or tried it before doesn't make it bad.

GRADUATE, CRIMINAL JUSTICE/POLITICAL SCIENCE/HISTORY, INDIANA UNIVERSITY—BLOOMINGTON

DON'T GET ARRESTED.

SENIOR, FINANCE, MIAMI UNIVERSITY

Buy a 24-hour planner. Trust me, it'll be the best $25 you spend each year.

JUNIOR, BIOLOGY AND NUCLEAR MEDICINE, UNIVERSITY OF THE INCARNATE WORD

Customize your education to something that you will enjoy. No one else will tell you how to make the best out of your education—you have to do that yourself! **FIGURE OUT WHAT YOU LIKE TO STUDY AND SPEND FOUR YEARS STUDYING IT!**

GRADUATE, POLITICAL SCIENCE, UNIVERSITY OF CALIFORNIA—SAN DIEGO

College is hard, kids. **KEEP YOUR HEAD LOW AND GO AT IT.**

JUNIOR, PHILOSOPHY, NORTHWESTERN UNIVERSITY

25 LAST WORDS

Now is your time to live.

SENIOR, ANTHROPOLOGY AND INTERNATIONAL STUDIES,
NORTHWESTERN UNIVERSITY

College is about having fun, more than anything, so if there is an opportunity to have a great experience with cool people, do it! Homework can always wait!

SENIOR, POLITICAL SCIENCE, RUTGERS—THE STATE UNIVERSITY OF NEW JERSEY

DON'T PAY ATTENTION TO WHAT OTHERS SAY. FIND YOURSELF. FIND OUT WHAT *YOU* FEEL IS RIGHT AND WHAT MAKES YOU HAPPY.

GRADUATE, PSYCHOLOGY, FLORIDA INTERNATIONAL UNIVERSITY

Honestly, one of the most vindicating things about school is looking back and remembering that you did have days in your life when pizza and PlayStation were more important than anything else. There will not be another time in your life when you get to do this.

GRADUATE, ANTHROPOLOGY, ARIZONA STATE UNIVERSITY

LAST WORDS

While in college, you mature and grow outside the classroom far more than you grow inside the classroom. The relationships you make and the people you meet will be the memories that you carry with you forever. **IT'S NOT HOW YOU STUDIED FOR THAT BIG TEST, IT'S HOW YOU AND YOUR FRIENDS WERE ABLE TO DRIVE TO ATLANTIC CITY THE NIGHT BEFORE THE TEST, AND STUDY ON THE WAY THERE AND BACK, AND STILL DO FINE ON THE EXAM.**

GRADUATE, BIOLOGY/NUTRITIONAL SCIENCES, PENNSYLVANIA STATE UNIVERSITY

College in general was a great and memorable experience. **I wish I could start all over again.**

SENIOR, PRE-LAW/MASS COMMUNICATIONS, OHIO STATE UNIVERSITY